Post-Comedy

Theory Redux series
Series editor: Laurent de Sutter

Published Titles
Mark Alizart, *Cryptocommunism*
Armen Avanessian, *Future Metaphysics*
Franco Berardi, *The Second Coming*
Alfie Bown, *The Playstation Dreamworld*
Alfie Bown, *Post-Comedy*
Laurent de Sutter, *Narcocapitalism*
Diedrich Diederichsen, *Aesthetics of Pop Music*
Roberto Esposito, *Persons and Things*
Boris Groys, *Becoming an Artwork*
Graham Harman, *Immaterialism*
Helen Hester, *Xenofeminism*
Srećko Horvat, *The Radicality of Love*
Lorenzo Marsili, *Planetary Politics*
Fabian Muniesa, *Paranoid Finance*
Dominic Pettman, *Infinite Distraction*
Eloy Fernández Porta, *Nomography*
Mikkel Bolt Rasmussen, *Late Capitalist Fascism*
Gerald Raunig, *Making Multiplicity*
Helen Rollins, *Psychocinema*
Avital Ronell, *America*
Nick Srnicek, *Platform Capitalism*
Grafton Tanner, *Foreverism*
Oxana Timofeeva, *Solar Politics*
Alenka Zupančič, *Disavowal*

Post-Comedy

Alfie Bown

polity

Copyright © Alfie Bown 2024

The right of Alfie Bown to be identified as Author of this Work has been asserted in accordance with the UK Copyright, Designs and Patents Act 1988.

First published in 2024 by Polity Press

Polity Press
65 Bridge Street
Cambridge CB2 1UR, UK

Polity Press
111 River Street
Hoboken, NJ 07030, USA

All rights reserved. Except for the quotation of short passages for the purpose of criticism and review, no part of this publication may be reproduced, stored in a retrieval system or transmitted, in any form or by any means, electronic, mechanical, photocopying, recording or otherwise, without the prior permission of the publisher.

ISBN-13: 978-1-5095-6338-8 (hardback)
ISBN-13: 978-1-5095-6339-5 (paperback)

A catalogue record for this book is available from the British Library.

Library of Congress Control Number: 2024937222

Typeset in 12.5 on 15pt Adobe Garamond
by Cheshire Typesetting Ltd, Cuddington, Cheshire
Printed and bound in Great Britain by CPI Group (UK) Ltd, Croydon

The publisher has used its best endeavours to ensure that the URLs for external websites referred to in this book are correct and active at the time of going to press. However, the publisher has no responsibility for the websites and can make no guarantee that a site will remain live or that the content is or will remain appropriate.

Every effort has been made to trace all copyright holders, but if any have been overlooked the publisher will be pleased to include any necessary credits in any subsequent reprint or edition.

For further information on Polity, visit our website: politybooks.com

Contents

Introduction: The Tension of Comedy	1
A Reactionary and a Liberal walk into a bar . . .	7
The Ideology of Laughing Freely	12
Didactic or Retroactive Laughter	16
The Form of Jokes	23
Despicable Jokes and the Ideology of Exception	30
Anxiety and Laughter	38
Sneezing Corpses	45
Satire and Satiation from Brexit to Trump '24	57
Memes and Group Psychology	69

CONTENTS

Keks and LOLs: Playground Humour	79
Milk Pouring and Trolling: Perverse, Psychotic, Neurotic	87
Activist or Fetishist	98
Dancing Laughter and Clowns from St Vitus to TikTok	108
Conclusion: Jokes, Masters and Orgasms	114
Bibliography	129

Introduction: The Tension of Comedy

At the most infamous of Oscars ceremonies, Will Smith and Chris Rock, two men famous for their harsh and cutting comedy, had a spat on a stage that is itself renowned for its 'roasting' humour. Despite this context, it provoked personal and social anxiety among those on stage and those off it. Today, comedy is fraught with tension like never before. We often hear the claim that no one can take a joke anymore, but what if we really can't take jokes anymore?

Not so long ago, comedy and laughter were a shared experience of relief – as Freud famously argued. At their best, ribbing, roasting, piss-taking and insulting were the foundation of a kind of universal culture – from the market-places of the medieval period to the playgrounds of the twentieth century – from which friend-ship, camaraderie and solidarity could emerge. To laugh together was, quite materially, the first step in the formation of society. Perhaps then, if we can't take a joke anymore, we also won't be able to build a society.

This book argues that laughter, as a shared communal experience of connection between people across divides and personal subjectivities becomes eroded by a particularist and identar-ian dynamic of contemporary capitalism. Joking together – and with and at each other – was once a key part of public life, which allowed a 'com-mons' to exist and universal solidarity to emerge, but now – with the privatization and commodifi-cation of every space – no such public exists, and no such laughter takes place. The kind of comedy that dominates in its place is not universalist rib-bing but self-congratulatory and smug satire and critique. We are, in this sense, living in a post-comedy world.

Comedy has become a pressure point for con-temporary culture. It flares up debates about censorship, cancellation, progressivism and even fascism (fascism and comedy of course have a long history). While commentators – and comedians themselves – are invariably tempted onto one side of this culture war, by being so they preclude the possibility of comedy working against the identity categories of contemporary capitalism and of the universal fraternal solidarity that marks true comedy. It is this missing universalist spirit of comedy that is at risk of becoming a thing of the past. If true comedy is defined by anything, it is by its ability to confront us with a deeply psychoanalytic realization – that we are all lacking subjects with failure at our core. True comedy, in this sense, is antithetical to the values of contemporary capitalism – and is under threat.

It wouldn't be difficult to claim the contrary: that comedy is everywhere and has never been more central to social life than it is now. From viral memes to endless laughing emojis to the increase in comedians made possible by the replacement of traditional comedy venues with social media spaces and the rise in short-form content embodied by TikTok, comedy conditions the rhythms of everyday life like never before. Yet, these proliferating forms of fragmented humour are productive of a private or privatized laughter that is symptomatic of the replacement of public space with a private social world of individuals as commodities in competition with each other. At the same time, the comedians at the top of the box office are more oppositional than ever. The fraternal comedy of solidary has been replaced by the enemy-making humour of identity. Instead of showing the lack at the core of subjectivity, comedy has become capitalist in that it disavows this universal lack and creates an illusion that some of us are complete and authentic subjects who are in the right, while others are lacking and nefarious subjects who are in the wrong.

Though it does not do justice to his thesis, Henri Bergson wrote that laughter can often issue from the subject whose feathers are thoroughly unruffled. In other words, laughter serves to secure the already established position of those doing the laughing. It seems now that this kind of laughter is the only kind that remains. But we can go further. By appearing as an instinctive response to things (we 'can't help' laughing), laughter seems to perceive a kernel of truth in the content of the joke or observation, thus validating the ideological position of the comedy. Laughter in this sense has a particularly 'retroactive' power to re-establish and entrench ideological positions. After laughing, the object of laughter acquires a special status, an appearance of truth, which seems to have pre-existed the joke.

Didactic humour has become the rule rather than the exception, and it characterizes both sides of the debate about comedy and 'woke' culture into which discussions of humour have been forced. James Acaster's viral jokes at the expense of Ricky Gervais and Dave Chappelle's perceived transphobia in fact operate in much the same way as the geriatric outspoken free speech activist John Cleese imagines the remake of Fawlty Towers to function. While one supports ideas of woke liberal culture and the other claims to rail against it with its anti-wokeness, both operate didactically to affirm the unruffled politics of the laughing subject.

The 'woke'/'anti-woke' discourses around comedy, or those that centre the discussion around free speech and censorship, end up obscuring the really important point about comedy today: its transformation in contemporary capitalization. Both sides of the culture war around comedy (the free speech brigade and the

INTRODUCTION

cancel culture no platformers) end up contributing to the mystification of what is really changing in our relationship to laughter and comedy (and by proxy to our relationships with each other) as new forms of digital capitalism restructure the public spaces that are defined by humour. To see what is happening with comedy, we need to be neither woke nor anti-woke, but anti-capitalist.

In short, this book shows that comedy confronts us with the lack at the heart of subjectivity. Revealing this lack operates in a universalist way: it connects us to each other, whether we are male, female, enby, black, white, intersectional, populist, Left or Right. The reason that comedy reveals lack is because it produces identities in relation to it and helps us deal with the anxiety of it. Laughter (hence its link with anxiety) helps us create and establish ideologies. Today, it is helping us to entrench divisive capitalist ideology. However, because laughter is tarrying with and dealing with ideology coming into being, it nevertheless cannot help but remind us of this lack from which we all – universally – originate. Jokes, then, create ideology – and identity – but they also remind us of contingency. In this sense, they won't be assimilated into the contemporary capitalism of identity politics. While there are many – comedians included – taking us into a didactic post-comedy world of opposition, comedy itself fights back in the service of universalist solidarity.

A Reactionary and a Liberal walk into a bar . . .

Acaster and Gervais are an introductory case in point of what is happening with comedy today. They vied with each other for the most streamed comedian on Netflix in 2022, while each took a strong position on either side of the culture war. Gervais represented free-speech advocates and brought transgender people into the content of his sets to embody the enemy of contemporary liberal culture, while Acaster appointed himself the defender of marginalized groups by characterizing Gervais as the apparently fascist enemy. Both achieved unprecedented commercial success (with Gervais selling the most tickets ever for a single gig in 2023) because both of these positions are well rewarded by the contemporary market.

But the success of these comedians (bolstered by the digital platform of Netflix) suggests not that comedy is alive and well, but that identity politics (as well as those who market themselves as for and against it) are a symptom of contemporary capitalism that suits its market. While both sides of the debate frame themselves as the dissident progressive non-normative force (as comedy has always tended to do), this didactic identitarian comedy both serves and is symptomatic of contemporary capitalism. While comedy has perhaps always been prey to the market, now political and cultural positions are commodified and the 'correct' positions are sold to us as products we're compelled to buy with our laughter. By this logic the test of a good joke is not whether people laugh at it but whether they agree with it.

Jesse David Fox, in his *Comedy Book: How Comedy Conquered Culture*, used the term 'post-comedy' to refer to jokes or comedy in which the comedian doesn't aim to provoke laughter in the audience and notes that such post-comedies can be more like TED talks than stand-up.

Two Donald Trump jokes – one from the Left and one from the Right – both viral in the last two years, show this didactic humour in full swing. In the first, a brave man sees a child about to be devoured by a lion after straying into the enclosure at the zoo. The man, who wears a MAGA hat, jumps in and throws the child to safety before punching the lion in the face. Afterwards he is interviewed by a nearby journalist and is excited to read about his heroism in the newspaper the next day, only to wake up to the headline: 'Right-wing fascist extremist punches African immigrant and steals his lunch.' In the second joke, Trump chats about foreign policy to his aide. 'The more immigrants we let in the better', he says. Seeing his gaff, the aide corrects him, 'the fewer'. Trump replies: 'I told you not to call me that yet.'

The jokes take opposing positions: one critiquing the tendency of liberal media to escalate every act by a Republican to a fear of rising fascism and the other criticizing the Republican tendency to sneak further towards fascism. In both cases, the didactic and moralistic joke secures the position of the subject laughing from the 'correct' position against the impure or corrupt other. Like Acaster and Gervais, they are two sides of the same coin.

Contrary to this, a laughter of solidarity might work, not to entrench us in our ideological positions but to universalize us and reveal our shared subjectivity. Though Freud is the theorist of comedy most known for ideas of laughter as a release of social repression, it is the Russian Marxist Mikhail Bakhtin who developed these ideas into a universalist 'laughter of all the people' (Bakhtin 1984, 12). Contrary to the laughter of superiority, this laughter can function as a kind of carnivalesque confrontation with one's own inadequacies and failures. In this laughter, kings become peasants and Left becomes Right. While the market competition of capitalism wants to stress our differences, this laughter shows our connectedness.

Though it often emerges without form and in spontaneity, a third joke might give us a sense of how this universalist humour could emerge. Jacques Derrida is rumoured to have enjoyed a joke that has been retold by various philosophers since and used to make a range of points. In the joke, a rabbi, a businessman and a cleaner are performing their lack of worth in the eyes of God. The businessman and the rabbi take it in turns to stand up and declare that they are unworthy. When it is the turn of the cleaner, he also stands up and declares himself worthless. Then, the businessman turns to the rabbi and says 'Who is that guy who dares to claim that he is nothing too!'

The message of the joke is that we are all human, whether rabbi, businessman or cleaner, and we all have a shared subjective structure. The joke points out that the rich will commoditize anything, even nothing. It is this nothing that we all share as subjects, despite our attempts to stress our differences, and comedy reminds us of it. In a carnival recognition of this universality, solidarity can emerge. In such collective experiences, it is not so much the content of jokes that is political (as it is with the question of whether Dave Chapelle is transphobic, etc., which has focused our attention so much in recent discussions), as it is of whether it creates a space for this formally transgressive experience of a universalizing shared laughter between individuals.

Jela Krečič argues that for thousands of years comedy has played a function of relieving tension but now comedy has become the source of tension. We can go one step further and say that laughter's tension needs to be seen in the context of the material conditions of capitalism and its privatization of public space. In other words, the reason why comedy causes tension today is that the world around it has become more divisive, while comedy remains unifying. Comedy can be the bastion of public life – at times the last thing left in a privatized world – and, if it can be recovered, a public 'commons' that cuts against identity politics might still be possible. At the moment, however, it is oppositional jokes – on all sides of a culture war – that are winning out over truly revolutionary comedy.

The Ideology of Laughing Freely

Comedy ought to be defined by its ability to change things – our perceptions of the world, the content of our jokes, the relations between ourselves and others – but didactic instances of laughter – which are perhaps forced and not genuinely funny – serve only to reaffirm the status of things as they are.

Laughter can sometimes seem to be the act of a most secure individual, a Hobbesian 'glory' of self-celebration. It can also, since it is a group activity, be what Jonathan Hall calls a 'fascist joy' involving 'collaboration with the powerholders' (Hall 1995, 17). It has been argued, as recently as 2022, that racist jokes fuel racism and, of course, they can do so within certain contexts (Pérez 2022). But, there is a difference between a racist joke and a racist statement.

The history of theorizing the cruel jokes of racism, for instance, has its roots in Hobbesian ideas of a laughter of superiority. Following this, Charles Baudelaire writes that when we see a man fall over in the street we issue a sudden and irrepressible laugh that seems to say 'Look at me! I am not falling! I am walking upright. I would never be so silly as to fail to see a gap in the pavement, or a cobblestone blocking the way' (Baudelaire 2006, 152). In this sense, it is when we laugh that we are caught in the trap of ideology, encouraged to take a position that then appears to be validated by the laughter itself. For Mladen Dolar:

> Laughter is the condition of ideology. It provides us with the distance, the very space in which ideology can take its full swing. It is only with laughter that we become ideological subjects . . . It is only when we laugh and breathe freely that ideology truly has a hold on us. (Dolar 1986, 307)

In this sense, a racist joke is more powerful than a racist statement, because it operates with the

THE IDEOLOGY OF LAUGHING FREELY

full swing of ideology, asserting a position and entrenching it, even making it appear to us that we have a natural or instinctive connection with the truth asserted in the joke. Though a self-proclaimed anti-racist, James Acaster, the comedian perhaps most associated with 'progressive' values today, can be seen in precisely this way: ideologically asserting the values of the day and using humour to naturalize them. His most famous Brexit joke is a case in point:

> 'In and out', it's a very hard decision. It's like the other day, my flatmate was making me a peppermint tea, and he said 'would you like bag leaving in, or taken out?' If you leave the bag in, on the whole the cup of tea itself will get stronger, and it might appear that the bag is getting weaker, but it's now part of a stronger cup of tea. Whereas if you take the bag out, the tea's now quite weak, but the bag itself goes directly in the bin.

The message is simple: Brexit Britain can be simplified to the point that the country is stronger in the EU than out of it. Those unable to see this are making an elementary mistake as foolish as taking a tea bag out of a cup of peppermint tea. For Acaster, the answer is obvious, and the joke is designed to point to the stupidity of the Brexit voter. Similarly, the Australian comedian Jim Jefferies, once known for his outspokenness, turned his comedy to target white nationalism after around 2016. For example:

> Why do White Supremacists always carry torches? You claim to be the master race and you're still using fire to illuminate things.

> The truth is that in the last nine years, right-wing militias have been responsible for twice as many terrorist attacks as Islamic extremists, so white people are actually better at terrorism – but it's not a competition.

One might easily object that this joke isn't funny, but it is nevertheless met by peals of laughter, forced or otherwise – online and in person – among the liberal communities among whom it gained traction in the Trump years. The laughter, issued by the crowd, appears to respond spontaneously to the apparent truth of the joke, to the supposed fact that it proves the medieval backwardness of the white supremacist in comparison

THE IDEOLOGY OF LAUGHING FREELY

with the superior wizened position of the more educated and evolved progressive who does the laughing. The important point here is the false equation between laughter and freedom, which is an assumption that conditions the very experience of laughing. As Dolar says, it is when we experience laughter as if it represents freedom that we are most in the grip of ideology. Even further, it might be said that laughter naturalizes and entrenches ideological positions, enshrining them as if they are truths. In this sense, there are no more ideological jokes than those of Acaster and Jefferies. The laughter that follows them has a kind of Dunning-Kruger effect, where a self-assessment takes place in which objectivity is eschewed and the position of the subject is confirmed in its validity. These moments embody the particularly divisive ideology of contemporary online discourse, defined by bubbles of self-confirming identitarianism. Such jokes are also perfectly fit for the short-form sharing on social media platforms among these communities, on which they rely for their success as a commodity.

Didactic or Retroactive Laughter

This powerful ideological comedy, its naturalizing force and ability to construct truths which it appears only to perceive, is also its radical or subversive edge. In fact, try as Acaster and Jeffries might to use comedy to confirm our biases and ideological positions, laughter seems to stretch further and to produce something more threatening to us – whether we like it or not. In his fifth seminar 'The Formations of the Unconscious', given between 1957 and 1958, the psychoanalyst Jacques Lacan pointed out that a history of associating comedy with superiority might miss the point. While many before him had seen laughter as the assertion of one group over another, Lacan felt something more at play in every laugh.

> If the [joke] evokes a feeling of superiority in us, which is entirely doubtful, it is surely much inferior in this respect. I am alluding here to one of the mechanisms that have often been unduly elevated to the origin of comical phenomena, namely, the feeling of superiority over others. This is entirely questionable. Although it was a very great mind

who attempted to sketch out the mechanism of the comic in this sense, namely Lipps, it's entirely refutable that this is where the essential pleasure of the comic lies. If there is anyone who happens to retain his superiority intact, it is our character, who possibly finds on this occasion a reason for his disappointment that is far from wounding his unshakeable confidence in himself. If any feeling of superiority takes shape [. . .], it acts more like a lure. Everything momentarily engages you in the mirage created by the way you situate the person who is recounting the story, or situate yourself, but what is going on here goes well beyond this. (Lacan 2017, 5, 128)

Lacan quotes Theodor Lipps and may in fact be slightly ungenerous to him in associating him with the idea of humour as giving rise to superiority. In fact, Lipps wrote in 1896 that the comic was the opposite of the feeling of superiority:

The comic ends in the moment when we ascend the pedestal again, i.e. where we begin to feel superior. The feeling of superiority proves to be the complete opposite of the feeling of the comic, as its classic deadly enemy. The feeling of the comic is

DIDACTIC OR RETROACTIVE LAUGHTER

> possible to the extent that the feeling of superiority doesn't arise and cannot arise. (Lipps 2005, 22)

This might lead us to consider comedy as related to carnival. For Bakhtin, the experience of laughter is a universalist eradication of all structure and hierarchy: ultimately against the kings and queens of superiority and in the service of the joyful relativity of everything and everyone.

> It is, first of all, a festive laughter. Therefore it is not an individual reaction to some isolated 'comic' event. Carnival laughter is the laughter of all the people. Second, it is universal in its scope; it is directed at all and everyone, including the carnival's participants. The entire world is seen in its droll aspect, in its gay relativity. Third, this laughter is ambivalent: it is gay, triumphant, and at the same time mocking, deriding. It asserts and denies, it buries and revives. (Bakhtin 1984, 11)

The carnival dissolves structure and organization, 'while carnival lasts, there is no other life outside it'. It is 'the defeat of power, of earthly kings, of the earthly upper classes, of all that oppresses and restricts'. This might not be very far from

Lipps's observation that laughter opposes superiority: after the carnival, superiority and hierarchy resume their place after this temporary burst of joyful universalist imagination.

But, when we laugh together, the fun doesn't stop there. Comedy is not a futile or brief departure from norms, nor is it (worse still) a 'relief valve' that allows those ideologies to maintain their hold after the event of laughter. Instead, it can start social change and build a universal 'commons' from which revolution can begin. Even anecdotally we can speak to the truth of this idea. Sitting across the table on a date, meeting a new work colleague for the first time, or even sitting with estranged family at Christmas dinner, the first laugh is not just a moment of relief but the start of something: a moment that makes other things possible.

Reading Dostoevsky, Bakhtin says that carnival 'absolutizes nothing, but rather proclaims the joyful relativity of everything' (Bakhtin 2004, 36) This is the critical point: in carnival, nothing essential or absolute is liberated or released. It is not about freedom and liberation of the ideological kind identified by Dolar. Instead, carnival is de-essentializing because it shows that everything is relative; neither the expressions of carnival celebration nor the cultural norms they oppose are privileged or absolute. When we are in the throes of carnival, we behave differently to normal, but this behaviour feels and appears just as possible, even just as natural, as does the behaviour of our everyday lives. Drag culture and transvestitism would be comparable experience. In other words, this laughter (and perhaps all laughter) shows us that structures exist, but that they do not pre-exist.

One misconception that conditions how we see and experience laughter is that comedy is the opposite of the serious. We see it as light, unsubstantial and even apolitical. On the contrary, laughter is a very significant event. There is an entire genre of philosophy that deals with the concept of the *event*, and the most important are the ideas of the French Marxist psychoanalyst Alain Badiou. Despite the fact that Badiou would never consider laughter to be an event in his own terms, it's possible that we could see each and every laugh as a kind mini/micro event.

Following Badiou, Slavoj Žižek usefully defines the event as 'the effect that seems to exceed its causes' (Žižek 2014, 5). An 'event' is a moment of excess, so that, while it has political stimuli, it also establishes new causes for itself, its effects retroactively restructuring the past into a new structure and bringing us within this reordered world, whether we like it or not. A major war that transforms a society would be one example. Falling in love would be one individual example, after which the entire world can only be seen through the lens of the event. In the sense that laughter is an effect that exceeds its causes, it is precisely such a phenomenon, something quite literally caused (often by a joke, for example) but which also restructures the situation into which it erupts.

Ian Parker traces the idea of event to the psychoanalytic idea of retroactivity or *nachträglichkeit*. This is a peculiarly psychoanalytic conception of time, a looping back and activation of what has already occurred, and the investment of that first event with a significance that turns it into what it will later always already be (Parker and Pavon-Cuellar 2013, 338). To give a simple example, the following simple joke is very commonly told in Jewish communities and has a long recurring history:

How many Jewish mothers does it take to change a lightbulb?

> That's OK, don't trouble yourself, we'll sit in the dark.

The joke is a typical example of the humour of stereotyping. On the one hand, it refers to the reality it appears to perceive: the fact that Jewish mothers are self-sacrificial and prone to complaining about it. On the other, its repetitious telling along with many versions of the same punchline (many similar jokes are made in The Sopranos about Italian mothers, for instance) creates the stereotype which it appears to respond to. It is quite literally impossible to know whether the stereotype or joking about it come first historically, and it is clear that there is a self-aware evolution of the idea along with humour about it. All nationalism jokes may do the same thing. There is no way of expressing the differences between the British and the French, for instance, except through humour, since it has always been the mechanism through which those identities are constructed in complementary opposition to each other. The jokes are as old as the national identity itself. Quite simply, these jokes produce ideas that appear to have pre-existed the jokes about them.

The Form of Jokes

These jokes take us closer to the more controversial topic of racist jokes, or jokes which attack minority or underprivileged groups. These often appear simply to serve the status quo. These jokes can seem like nothing more than collaboration with the powerholders and, with the retroactive power of jokes in mind, they may be even more dangerous than this in their ability to produce, naturalize and entrench prejudices. However, the question of whether we can separate racist jokes from antiracist ones is a complicated one.

It has certainly been tried before. In his book on humour Simon Critchley writes that 'it is important to recognize that not all humour is [liberating], and most of the best jokes are fairly reactionary or, at best, simply serve to reinforce social consensus'. Thus, for Critchley, as for many other joke theorists, there are two types of joke; the reactionary on the one hand and the radical or liberatory on the other. On the other hand, the German–Jewish Marxist Walter Benjamin had always argued to the contrary, writing in *The Origin of German Tragic Drama* that 'the cruel joke is just as original as harmless mirth' (Benjamin 2009, 127).

The Czech writer Milan Kundera wrote that 'imitation of laughter and (the devil's) original laughter are both called by the same name', which seems both to separate and connect the apparently different forms of laughter. Perhaps Kundera's phrasing touches on a clue to the connection between racist and antiracist laughter and jokes. When the laughter is repetitious and imitative – repeated and chortled at in didactic agreement – it is racist and ideological. Yet, at the same time and in the same jokes and the same laugh is a much more diabolical potential: the antiracist laughter that undoes ideology and confronts us with the universal lack it covers up. A famous – often repeated – Jewish joke illustrates this doubleness:

'Did you hear about the Jews that sunk the Titanic?'
'Jews? I thought that was an iceberg.'
'Goldberg, Steinberg, Rosenberg, what's the difference?'

It is, on the surface, a racist joke, which speaks to the stereotypes around naming and the idea of blaming Jewish people for a myriad of problems. But that is clearly only part of the story. One imagines two antisemites – perhaps in a bar – having the exchange. For Todd McGowan, this joke is antiracist and in fact he argues that it embodies the antiracist potential of jokes:

> The significance of this joke lies in its ability to focus on the form that produces racism no matter what its content. Here, we see how supposed racial difference can be equated to words rhyming. It is nothing more substantial than that. By shifting people's focus from content to form, the antiracist joke works psychically against the power of the racist fantasy, which relies on people not recognizing form. (McGowan 2022, 36)

For McGowan, content is shown to be less important than form, and making this realization is profoundly antiracist because racism relies on ignoring the importance of form and believing in the primacy of content: black people really are bad fathers, Jewish people really are thrifty, etc., etc. McGowan – both here and in his book on comedy – sees comedy as functioning both for good and for ill, just as Critchley does. Following

Dolar's warning about laughter being experienced as liberatory and free, he argues that 'comedy has the potential to act as a site for radical emancipatory politics, but it can just as easily function in the most ideological fashion in the guise of radicality' (McGowan 2017, 18). In fact, McGowan goes as far as to identify some jokes as antiracist – like the one above – and others as racist:

> Kant includes a racist joke at the expense of an Indian in the 1790 *Critique of the Power of Judgment*. The joke goes as follows: 'If someone tells this story: An Indian, at the table of an Englishman in Surat, seeing a bottle of ale being opened and all the beer, transformed into foam, spill out, displayed his great amazement with many exclamations, and in reply to the Englishman's question "What is so amazing here?" answered, "I'm not amazed that it's coming out, but by how you got it all in", we laugh, and it gives us a hearty pleasure: not because we find ourselves cleverer than this ignorant person, or because of any other pleasing thing that the understanding allows us to note here, but because our expectation was heightened and suddenly disappeared into nothing.' Even though Kant claims here that the ignorance of the Indian is not the

source of the humour in the joke, it is nonetheless part of the enjoyment that the joke delivers for Kant, which is the index of its racism. (McGowan 2022, 211)

Contrary to McGowan's instinct to divide racist from antiracist jokes, and perhaps even contrary to Kant's argument that there is a difference between the racism and the source of the humour in the joke, the important point is that the joke doesn't work without its racism, and its proximity to racism is the core of its antiracism. By moving its audience towards the possibly of a racist joke – as Kant says 'our expectation was heightened' – and then pivoting 'suddenly' to a more innocent one – it forces the audience into the antiracist realization that the structure is more important than its content. In this sense, the joke is a better example of McGowan's argument about anti-racist jokes than his own example.

The conclusion here might be that it is not so much that there are two possible readings of the joke – one racist and one antiracist – but that it is only by being racist that the joke can be antiracist. A more modern version of Kant's joke might be the following common dad joke:

THE FORM OF JOKES

> What do you call a Black man walking on the moon? The answer: An astronaut.

By pivoting the content, the form becomes visible and makes an antiracist point, not so much by tricking the audience into revealing their prejudice – as the typical reading would be (the dads telling the joke often respond by saying 'aha, got you!') – but by revealing jokes themselves to be complicit in the construction of racism (rather than reflective of it) in the first place. Even a joke with completely innocuous content – far away from race or nationalist – can have this effect, for instance the classic Tommy Cooper line:

> What do you call a fish with no eyes? A fsh.

For McGowan, 'when we laugh at comic moments, we enjoy the contradictory form of our excess and implicitly grasp its connection to what we lack. The contradictory nature of our subjectivity marks the birth of comedy' (McGowan 2017, 18). By grasping our own lacking subjectivity, our own foolishness and incompleteness, we face the universal nature of our lacking subjectivities. To do so is profoundly antiracist, whether

29

the topic of race is on the table or not. We can add to McGowan's argument that rather than some jokes being racist and others antiracist, this de-essential thinking inherent to the joke – and perhaps to all jokes – is their radical core. In fact, it is only by being essentialist, racist or ideological that it can be de-essentialist and antiracist.

Despicable Jokes and the Ideology of Exception

Compared with McGowan quoting from Kant in the footnotes of a philosophy book, there are many more clearly racist jokes and jokes deemed culturally unacceptable and impermissible. At the moment, jokes about the transgender community are those that catch the most cultural attention. Despite the temptation to shy away from such jokes, it might be worth thinking about whether there isn't nevertheless a radical grain of antiracism or of universalism even in these seemingly despicable instances of humour. For example, some that were published in a relatively soft 2023 joke book for 'politically incorrect' readers who watch populist British online news networks:

Q: What is the biggest day of confusion in Oakland, California?
A: Father's Day.

The joke is predictably racist, turning on the idea of promiscuous men in the black community. Though it's the kind of joke one could imagine told by a white British dad about his counterparts, its often found that such jokes are told more by their own communities than by those laughing at them. Corliss Outley, for instance, has shown how the black community use 'racist' jokes as a coping mechanism, and how there is a history of doing so that entered a new phase during the Covid-19 pandemic (Outley 2021, et al.). Sometimes the argument is posited that only members of those communities themselves have the right to joke about their own communities and identities, but this risks further particularizing and moving away from the universalist potential of comedy. It also supplements a division of society into the sort of filter bubbles encouraged by the curation of digital media feeds. Curated jokes for particular audiences play a key role in these spaces, with each group joking only to their own and with their own.

One of the more controversial jokes of recent years has been British comedian Ricky Gervais's jokes about the transgender community. Gervais started his Netflix special set with the 'Oh, women!', as if he was going to follow the well-trodden format of men complaining about women. He continues:

> Not all women, I mean the old-fashioned ones. The old-fashioned women, the ones with wombs. Those fucking dinosaurs. I love the new women. They're great, aren't they? The new ones we've been seeing lately. The ones with beards and cocks.

This joke was heavily criticized by some of the transgender community and by other observes, and it also fuelled responses from other comedians such as those of James Acaster discussed above. When put on the spot about it, Gervais had an interesting theory of comedy of his own to posit in his defence:

> That's when I say something I don't really mean, for comic effect, and you, as an audience, you laugh at the wrong thing because you know what the right thing is. It's a way of satirizing attitudes.

Gervais makes the point that in laughter associated with shock and transgression, laughter issues not only in cases of agreement with the transgressive joke but often against it. In this sense, laughter serves to reorient society around social and cultural issues: by laughing together, social norms can be established and points of anxiety can be approached and then dealt with in humour. Gervais might be right that as social change takes place – for instance in attitudes towards gender – comedy and laughter around the topic are not so much a backlash against this 'progressive' change (as the liberal critique of Gervais's apparently conservative humour claimed) but part of the resetting of social norms and convention in an evolving society. In this sense, as in others, laughter can be a foundational moment for the production of society.

Cancelling such comedy usually purports to be in order to protect us from becoming too divided from each other, since by cautioning against offending any of the groups that live together in multiculturalism we ward against setting groups against each other. On the contrary though, without this humour there can be no society and, instead, we remain particularist groups unaware of – and in denial of – our universalist connections.

Extending from this, there could be an even greater danger in disbarring the trans community from inclusion in jokes than by inviting them into the ribbing and roasting. By discouraging jokes about the trans community for instance, we risk partitioning them off from society as it forms and re-forms. By particularizing groups and not joking about them, they become completely alienated from the processes of society. Jim Jeffries – despite tending towards didactic comedy on the topic of politics – makes a very different joke that speaks to this:

> I can't empathize with trans people because I can't imagine being born in a body that disgusts me and that I don't want to have. Oh wait. That's 98% of us.

The joke could likely be read either as pro- or anti-trans, but it does at least attempt to invite transgender people into the processes of comedy and even – at the level of content – into a universalist way of thinking, where rather than being uniquely lacking as a subject, the audience is invited to see all subjects as universally lacking. One could object that the conflation of gender dysmorphia with feeling unattractive is unfair, but the spirit of the joke seems more of an invitation to be included than an impulse to oppositionalize.

American comedian Andrew Schulz makes a more ostensibly transphobic joke that can nevertheless be considered in these terms:

> Transgender bathrooms: it was a big thing to do, changing all the bathrooms. And trans people are only 0.1% of the population. Do you know what other group are 0.1% of the population? People with six fingers. We should change all gloves.

What seems like an invitation to laugh at transgender people for thinking themselves special and demanding disproportionate attention might – because of that – be an important critique of the capitalist invitation into the ideology of exception. The ideology of exception is the belief that the laws of the market don't apply to us. Ultimately, it is the deeply held fantasy that capitalism – or the reality principle – is not real or is not governing our position in the world.

DESPICABLE JOKES AND THE IDEOLOGY OF EXCEPTION

We all like to see ourselves as deserving of unique recognition, but this kind of capitalist recognition is always arbitrary and cannot be universally applied to all of its subjects at once, marking it as inherently unequal.

The identity politics approach to representation is a good example of the function of this ideology of exception as a support for capitalism. Often, we would rather celebrate the appointment of a female CEO than change the material conditions and redistribute wealth or power because it speaks to the fantasy that we could be the CEO, rather than the reality that it is always inevitable that the structure of capitalism ensures inequality. By inviting the comparison with gloves, Schulz's joke is not at the expense of trans people but at the expense of a system that sells us the ideology of exception but cannot provide universal recognition.

Another joke with the same structure is a popular 2023 TikTok snippet. In the clip, a Chinese girl explains to her American friend on arriving at the airport in China that people here can tell American–Chinese from Chinese–Chinese. She proceeds to identify types of Chinese subject in the airport:

DESPICABLE JOKES AND THE IDEOLOGY OF EXCEPTION

> Hong Kong–Chinese: Bluetooth. Shanghai–Chinese: Bougie. Taiwanese: weird but cute.

The American friend sees another group and asks, 'what kind of Chinese are they?' To which the Chinese girl replies:

> What the fuck are you talking about, do you want to get yourself cancelled? Those are Koreans. We can tell that because they all have the same face.

Here, the joke pivots the opposite way to the joke about the black astronaut on the moon. Instead of pivoting away from racism, it jumps to a more intense form, moving from a lighthearted stereotyping to a classic prejudice about other races looking the same. More importantly though, it presents the ideology of exception before showing it to be a fantasy. Like the idea of adding a sixth finger to every pair of gloves, it shows that while there is an illusion of an exception somewhere, there is always collateral damage or disregard somewhere else. Certain things might be picked out for exceptionalism, but this obscures the fact that it is the system itself that ensures a lack of universal recognition. In this sense, these are universalist jokes, which invite us to be joked about and included in the process of being unrecognized. The subjects in these examples – Korean and transgender people – are not ostracized by the jokes but invited into the universalist society of misrecognition that they reveal to us.

Anxiety and Laughter

We often tell jokes when we are feeling anxious or unsure of ourselves. As Ricky Gervais's amateur theorization of comedy suggests, it might be that laughter helps us deal with anxiety by re-directing it into the production of new norms. This has its roots in a history of associating laughter with anxiety and the connection is a key part of laughter's unique relationship to society and identity.

The psychoanalyst Charles Mauron is the first significant writer to link laughter directly to anxiety in his 1964 book *La Psychocritique du Genre Comique*. Mauron remarks that comedy is 'la *renversement* des situations d'angoisse' [the reversal of the situation of anxiety]. He sees comedy as a kind of safety mechanism for dealing with anxiety, arguing that comedy provides a release from psychic blockage and allows the laughing subject to deal with and solve psychic problems. There is a parallel between Mauron and the British philosopher Northrop Frye's comments on comedy, whose work is much more regularly quoted in discussions of comedy and laughter. For Frye 'psychologically [comedy] is like the removal of a neurosis or blocking point and the restoration of an unbroken current of energy' (Frye 1957, 172).

However, Mauron's describing the process of moving from anxiety to comedy as 'renversement' is important and it is more specific than Frye's rather general sense that comedy helps us deal with things. Renversement implies inverting or reverting one thing into something else, and OED retains a sense that renversement has been used historically as a synonym for metamorphosis. Renversement does not imply progress or development and, in this sense, it should be thought of like the Hegelian concept of *aufhebung*. Typically, *aufhebung* is that which happens when thesis and antithesis meet; and a traditional reading of Hegel might read the process in terms of a progress narrative, making *aufhebung* a triumph of the new over the old that needed overcoming. Yet, this is not the sense in which

Mauron – or Hegel – intended the process to be seen.

Mauron reads Thomas Hobbes's theory of laughter as against the grain, arguing that there is an inward dialectical movement in the subject, overturning earlier commentators who see Hobbes's thesis as evidence of the static and ahistorical ideology of hierarchical superiority and/or moral censure. Mauron works with the notion of the self's illusory superiority, which is only momentarily sustained against the perception of its own weakness and inferiority. Thus, if *aufhebung* can be read in these terms, it is not the totalizing motion of one thing dealing with another but a kind of trick, where something new is produced that appears to have a history behind it. This challenges the chronological sense that *aufhebung* produces because, in showing that structure coming into being, it indicates that it cannot have been there to govern that process, making it a kind of self-deception, something that has to hide where it comes from.

In this role, laughter functions to *give anxiety an object*. This is close to an argument about the relationship between anxiety and objects made by Sigmund Freud, though Freud did not connect anxiety to laughter, despite his lifelong interest in both topics separately. For early Freud, anxiety was caused by a non-normative interruption to the subject's development. He followed this idea that anxiety is the result of a blockage of some kind for some time, both in *The Interpretation of Dreams* and in *Three Essays on Sexuality* (Freud 2001, *SE* 4: 337–8, *SE* 7: 224).

However, in a letter to Fliess as early as 1897 Freud had written that he had 'decided henceforth to regard as separate factors what causes libido and what causes anxiety', suggesting that he already considered the view of anxiety as response or symptom to be problematic. By 1926 in *Inhibitions, Symptoms and Anxiety*, Freud's initial argument about anxiety had been turned fully on its head; rather than seeing anxiety as a response to other factors, anxiety itself takes up a position as primal. From this point, Freud begins to think about what anxiety causes, as much as he was preoccupied with what it is caused by.

In the essay Freud demonstrates that anxiety cannot be seen as an anxiety of something, opposing anxiety to 'fear' or 'phobia'. A phobia, Freud says, is formed as a response to an undirected and unexplainable more primary anxiety. The phobia has two effects. First, it 'avoids conflict due to ambivalence' by centring unplaced anxiety around an object (Freud 2001, *SE* 20: 125). Through this process 'an internal, instinctual danger' (that of unplaced anxiety) is replaced by an 'external, perceptual one' (that of fear directed at a particular object) (Freud 2001, *SE* 20: 126). To put it in general terms, when we become scared of something – and we are conscious of this fear – repression has occurred and anxiety can cease generating because we have something to orient it around. This object appears to be the cause of our fear, and in one sense it is, but is also the effect of our anxiety that has caused something which then appears to be itself a case.

Laughter can be seen to have exactly this retroactive power and to be a mechanism through which anxiety is given an object. The moment of laughter, then, is a moment of *aufhebung*, an 'event' that changes and shifts the structure of the subject. In its relation to anxiety, laughter establishes history, mooring unplaced anxiety into a structure of cause and effect, where a new object is established.

This laughter establishes a new history. This shows the creativity of laughter, or even the destructive creativity, for which even the smallest joke provides evidence. The moment of laughter is one in which cause and effect are established, but laughter shows us this – indicating that what is constructed as rational sense is not anchored or secured anywhere, and thus returning the subject not to the very anxiety from which it came but to new anxieties. Something has been changed, so that laughter shows us that history is not always the same history but something constantly changing. If laughter produces a history, a cause-and-effect structure, then it also shows that history is not stable but a constantly changing thing, always anxious for its own stability.

During the 1960s, Jacques Lacan developed Freud's theory of anxiety and connected it to one of his most important concepts: the *objet petit a*. He added to Freud's insight that although we are afraid 'of' something and our anxiety seems to be 'not without an object' (Freud 2001, S10: 77), the subject 'does not know what object is involved' even when it believes that it does (Freud 2001, S10: 77). The real 'something' that the subject is afraid of – underneath its external fear of spiders or immigrants, for example – is not an articulable object but is rather 'an object that is outside any possible definition of objectivity' (Freud 2001, S10: 75). Alenka Zupančič uses a joke to show this point in Lacan:

> A patient comes to [his analyst] complaining that a crocodile is hiding under his bed. During several sessions the analyst tries to persuade the patient that this is all in his imagination. A month later the analyst meets a friend, who is also a friend of his ex-patient, and asks him how the latter is. The friend answers: 'Do you mean the one who was eaten by a crocodile?'

For Zupančič, this joke shows us a critical insight about anxiety and illustrates the existence of the Lacanian idea of the *objet petit a*:

> The lesson of this story is profoundly Lacanian; if we start from the idea that anxiety does not have an object, what are we then to call this thing which killed, which 'ate' the subject? What is the subject telling the analyst in this joke? Nothing other than: 'I have the *objet petit a* under my bed; I came too close to it.'

In other words, every subject – of whatever race, gender, class or personal history – has a lack at their core that operates as an originary anxiety that continually generates and regenerates, threatening the stability of the subject. This universalist feature of subjectivity operates against those forces that attempt to divide subjects from each other. By remembering Charles Mauron's forgotten analysis of laughter and anxiety, what we can add to the developments from Lacan and Zupančič is that jokes themselves play a role in hiding this original anxiety from its subjects. Jokes turn us away from our universal anxiety and into fantasies of various kinds. Some of these fantasies might be gendered, nationalist, homophobic, or they may appear progressive and egalitarian. Jokes allow us to better handle our anxiety, and to repress it, but they also – because they are repetitious everyday occurrences – serve to remind us of it. In this way, we can understand how jokes operate both universally and in the service of particularist ideology – often at the same time.

Sneezing Corpses

This shows that all jokes, and all laughs – no matter how complicit and problematic they might seem – involve a kind of doubleness. Jokes about nationality are a case in point. The joke might reinforce a prejudice or superiority belief of one group over another, but it also reveals the construction of identity as based on the creation of otherness and the establishment of difference, which is demonstrated by the joke form itself. It is the form that is important rather than the content, so that the nationalities are interchangeable; the same jokes English people tell about Scottish people are told in Scotland about people from Aberdeen. The joke asserts an identity, but it also shows that identity for what it is, a structure created by an assertion of one thing in relation to another, constituting both things in the process and thereby showing that they do not pre-exist.

In other words, jokes might attempt to divide us, but they seem to want to unite us, whether we want them to or not. At the same time though, because comedy deals with anxiety, it can often be useful to repeatedly make jokes or to turn to humour at times when anxiety is at its highest. This can often be humorously visible when people recount comic tales or narrate events from their personal or anecdotal history with a comic tone, precisely when those tales or events touch upon a trigger for personal anxiety. We often turn to the comic when we approach our biggest anxieties. There is a fantastic example of this in one of the most well-known English novels, *Great Expectations* by Charles Dickens.

In the middle of the novel, the central character Pip makes a trip to see his friend Mr Wopsle – a terrible but ambitious actor – perform at the theatre. The chapter is often thought of as a kind of comic interlude from the main action (a fact that itself demonstrates that comedy is often dismissed as apolitical or digressive), as Pip attends the theatre under enormous pressure that his life will come undone by the reappearance of Magwitch, his criminal benefactor, who could undo his economic and social progress.

The episode provides us with important insight into the function of comic narration in relation to anxiety. Immediately switching to a comic tone, the chapter opens with a joke transporting the reader into the play:

> On our arrival in Denmark, we found the king and queen of that country elevated in two arm-chairs on a kitchen-table, holding a Court. The whole of the Danish nobility were in attendance; consisting

of a noble boy in the wash-leather boots of a gigantic ancestor, a venerable Peer with a dirty face who seemed to have risen from the people late in life, and the Danish chivalry with a comb in its hair and a pair of white silk legs, and presenting on the whole a feminine appearance. My gifted townsman stood gloomily apart, with folded arms, and I could have wished that his curls and forehead had been more probable.

As an instance of the tragic descending into comedy it may be comparable with the production put on by Bottom et al. in *A Midsummer Night's Dream*. It is a joke about the failure of the production to live up to the standards expected of a performance of *Hamlet*.

Turning *Hamlet* into comedy has a history that would eventually lead to Ernst Lubitsch's *To Be or Not to Be*, as well as the Mel Brooks version of the film. Dickens seems to have been absorbed in nineteenth-century popular culture performances of *Hamlet* as comedy. In *Great Expectations,* the playbill advertising the play gives Wopsle the name 'Roscius', which probably refers to William Henry Betty (1791–1874), who was so famous as to be called 'infant Garrick', 'infant Roscius', or

SNEEZING CORPSES

'young Roscius'. As a provincial actor he played Hamlet at Covent Garden Theatre (and later at Drury Lane) during the season of 1803–4, with the famous clown Joseph Grimaldi, whose memoirs Dickens edited in 1838, playing one of the grave diggers and offering comic renditions of various scenes to the play. In fact, several full-length comic versions of *Hamlet* appeared in the 1850s and 1860s, eventually including the popular anonymous production *A Thin Slice of Ham let!* of around 1863. There is something particularly funny about turning seriousness into farce.

In this instance, *Hamlet* is a document to copy as closely as possible and the performance is then judged against its ability to do this successfully, with laughter issuing at its failure. The perception of a failure can be the cause of laughter, but in this case it is the effects of the laughter that are more significant. In this, the most important thing is not what is happening on stage – the failure itself – but the relationship between the stage and the audience or, perhaps more importantly, between the events and Pip's narration of them.

Pip wishes Wopsle's performance could 'have been more probable' but his narration is already responsible for emphasizing the comedy of the

49

SNEEZING CORPSES

performance and for making the performance funnier for the reader. He uses techniques of incongruity, juxtaposing the 'king' and 'queen' with the 'kitchen-table' to place the nobility in a setting in which they are never found. He uses sarcasm, referring to the 'gifted townsman' whose appearance is 'improbable' and he employs a satirical mocking by exaggerating the limited number of actors and the poor quality of props that are supposed to represent 'the whole of the Danish nobility' but in fact amount to a man with a comb in his hair and white leggings and a 'venerable peer' who has neglected to wash his face, pointing humorously to the reduced-scale and amateur attempt to replicate the grandeur of *Hamlet*'s famous scene. Probably the funniest element of Pip's narration is the joke that this is so obviously a performance involving 'two arm-chairs on a kitchen-table' as a stand-in for a throne that the viewer cannot get lost in the production. This is contained in the chapter's opening line 'on our arrival in Denmark', a joke about being transported directly into the action of a performance that absolutely resists transporting the viewer into its world in any absorbing realist or cinematic way.

One Dickens critic inadvertently borrows Ricky Gervais's theory that when we laugh at the wrong thing we secure our shared sense of the right thing to analyse the scene. For James Kincaid, Pip has a 'very strong agreement' with a world order, which explains his laughter at this failure on stage (Kincaid 1971, 22). His can be seen as a directed laughter that distances the subject laughing from the target of the laughter, mocking the catastrophe and disorder on stage and showing a firm conviction in how things should be (i.e. how *Hamlet* ought to be performed).

Amidst the anxiety, the idea that it is those who are most secure who do the laughing seems fallible. When the ghost of Hamlet's father is plainly seen to be reading his lines from a script attached to his truncheon, Pip writes:

> The royal phantom also carried a ghostly manuscript round its truncheon, to which it had the appearance of occasionally referring, and that too, with an air of anxiety and a tendency to lose the place of reference which were suggestive of a state of mortality. It was this, I conceive, which led to the shade's being advised by the gallery to 'turn

over!' – a recommendation which it took extremely ill. (Dickens 2003, *GE*, 251)

While the audience begin to enjoy the play for what it has become (a kind of comic chaos), Pip continually emphasizes the fact that the laughter is directed firmly at the targets on stage. When the audience begin to shout from the stands the production appears to be moving towards destruction and chaos and the Bhaktinian 'carnival' breakdown of order begins to appear. However, Pip would have us believe that the audience's laughter is not in chaos and embracing disorder, as it would be in a moment of carnival, but directed at disorder. This directed laughter is neither a temporary departure from official order nor a complete rejection of it but a process that involves constructing the appearance that outside the play there is a solid agreement with a particular worldview. The laughter would then be more like what we might think of when it comes to modern stand-up comedy, where the audience is unified in its directed laughter at an agreed target.

Pip eventually feels he has succumbed to the temptation to laugh with and in the same way as the rest of the audience. He seems to have

SNEEZING CORPSES

been brought into the chaos of the moment and to embrace its infectious carnival-like laughter which it is 'hopeless' to resist:

> We had made some pale efforts in the beginning to applaud Mr Wopsle; but they were too hopeless to be persisted in. Therefore we had sat, feeling keenly for him, but laughing, nevertheless, from ear to ear. I laughed in spite of myself all the time, the whole thing was so droll.

This moment provides an interesting contradiction to Henri Bergson's claim that laughter requires an 'anaesthesia of the heart'. In his famous essay on laughter Bergson argues that laughter is usually accompanied with an 'absence of feeling', whereas here Pip's reluctant laughter is accompanied by serious pity for Wopsle. On the contrary, this laughter appears to be the act of someone much troubled and involved.

The experience of laughing seems to make Pip feel unruffled or to be a temporary letting go of any concerns, at least for the moment in which he laughs 'from ear to ear' as if giving up on a feeling of concern for Wopsle and embracing the infectious laughter of those around him.

53

For Alenka Zupančič, it can be when we feel most lost in comic chaos that we are in fact most grounded in rational order. In her article on the humour of the 'sneezing corpse' she discusses this idea in relation to watching theatre, arguing that we sometimes surrender to the chaos and disorder of the play in order to create 'the guarantee that outside the play there is a reality firmly in its place, a reality to which we can return (after the play, or at any moment if we choose to.)' Pip's final roars of apparently carnival laughter may be involved in something like this, enjoying the moment of chaos in order to guarantee a feeling of secure reality outside this temporary madness. in surrendering to the 'droll' chaos, Pip feels that outside all this nonsense his own reality is quite secure.

The reader may sense otherwise, detecting Pip's anxiety. Behind him in the theatre is Magwitch, the symbol of all he tries to repress, so that the retreat into comedy is a holding of anxiety at bay. Laughter is an assertion of our unruffledness or of our security, but it is often an anxious assertion that indicates how fragile we really are. The 'corpse' in Wopsle's production of Hamlet is not sneezing but it is coughing and Pip comments:

> Several curious little circumstances transpired as the action proceeded. The late king of the country not only appeared to have been troubled with a cough at the time of his decease, but to have taken it with him to the tomb, and to have brought it back.

The coughing or sneezing corpse is a familiar comic trope, and one which operates on the boundary between comedy and the uncanny. Robert Pfaller has produced the most comprehensive and convincing argument about the relationship, suggesting that 'the comic is what is uncanny for others'. (Pfaller 2005, 28). Pfaller uses an example given by Octave Mannoni of an actor playing dead on the stage, and suddenly sneezing. He explains that in order to laugh at the dead man sneezing, one has to know that the man is not really dead but an actor pretending to be dead, and one also has to imagine the possibility of someone else not realizing this, being deceived by the theatre and shocked by the sneeze. This imaginary 'naive observer' would certainly not be laughing but would find the incident properly uncanny. By laughing, we ensure that what could be uncanny is transformed into the humorous. In this sense it is reversal of anxiety into comedy, and we see a perfect example of it in *Great Expectations*. This comedy can approach the uncanny all – universally – failures, but it deals with it by re-inscribing a comforting distance between those who fail and those who are above it.

The uncanny is a reminder of the universal nature of subjectivity. As with the most classic example of the uncanny – the figure of the double, which is also a classic comic figure – we find it uncanny because it reveals to us that we are not unique and instead that we are nothing but subjects: that we are all just humans with a shared subjective structure. When we turn from this anxiety, and these potentially uncanny moments, turning them to comedy, we re-inscribe a difference between subjects by creating a naive observer who operates as a foil and allows us to perceive the world as if there is a difference between us and them, between those who understand the world as it is and those fools who cannot see the truth. This didactic version of humour is more dominant today than ever.

Satire and Satiation from Brexit to Trump '24

Like the Trump jokes discussed earlier, political jokes are a case in point of the attempt to turn jokes from a unifier into a divider, allowing the subject to move from an uncanny universalist confrontation with originary anxiety to a didactic belief in the us and them – the 'fear' of the Other – of the naive observer. For instance, in the 'most popular' Brexit joke according to *The Irish Times*:

> Why does the Brexiter have so many children?
> Because he refuses to acknowledge that pulling out never works.

The apparently simple joke plays on the idea that it could only be a detriment to 'pull out' of the EU and that those who would be foolish enough to think otherwise would be foolish enough to have medieval views about contraception. At a stretch, it might hint at the slightly more edgy idea of Brexiteers as being likely to have more children because of ideas of British tabloid readers and voters of nationalist parties as being prone to having children in order to claim benefits from the UK government. Thousands of such jokes were immensely common in the years running up to Brexit – and these anti-Brexit jokes were compiled and collected by most of the major Remain-focused news outlets in the UK and Ireland. They speak directly to the need to deal with anxiety by creating the naive observer whose stupidity secures our sense of things. In reality, no Brexiteer honestly supports the pulling out method of contraception, but it comforts the Remain voter to create the divisive idea that they might.

Perhaps in light of how laughter can invert (or *reinvert*) anxiety, it might be that we tell jokes, in particular the divisive political kind, in order to retroactively create an idea of a secure reality we can relate to. It is in the last fifty pages of his *Aesthetics* that Hegel discusses comedy most directly, but it is *The Logic of Sense* that explains his theory of how meaning is constructed in a deceptive trick between form and content. Here, he discusses the idea of origin or beginning, of any reality that exists in the world before it is understood by the interpretation of humans. 'Earlier abstract thought', he comments, is 'interested only in the principle as content.' Hegel departs from those looking for an originary content, which is represented by form, and instead posits that the very beginning is the intersection between form and content. A beginning 'is to be made' remarks Hegel, rather than pre-existing.

> There is nothing in heaven or nature or spirit or anywhere else that does not contain just as much immediacy as mediation, so that both these determinations prove to be unseparated and inseparable and the opposition between them nothing real. (Hegel 2010, 45–6)

The immediacy and its mediation are simultaneously produced, and they are separated not by something real but by a false appearance, which allows content to appear as something originary, which then exists as if 'to be represented'. Such interpretive moments have the retroactive quality that can be thought of as *aufhebung*, and it is this concept that inspired both Badiou's idea of event and Freud's concept of *nachträglichkeit*.

This interpretive gesture is exactly the one made by jokes. The trick that jokes play is what makes them ideological, but it is also where we find their subversiveness. The joke functions to create a false opposition between form and content, and this operates as its ideological component. While they also contain a dangerous and universalist reminder of this origin, political and social life seem dominated by jokes and humour intent on denying this and remaining on the side of didactic ideology. By creating meaning, a joke reminds us how political divisions and ideologies are constructed, but the joke about Brexiteers wants to appear as a form that refers to already existing content and plays a deceptive trick to do so.

Another good example of this kind of humour from the Brexit years is when the online comedian Matt Buck joined a KKK march playing ridiculous songs on a giant sousaphone. The comic – viral – act seemed to destroy the racist style and aesthetic of the march and British comedy show *The Last Leg* repeated the act by hounding conservative politician Jeremy Hunt with the instrument. This form of mockery seemed to embody the tactics of progressives at the time: from endless Trump mockery and political dank memes to witty protest boards, the 'progressive community' – perhaps in competitive response to the visceral humour of the Chan boards and right-leaning online communities – was laughing, or at least it claimed to be. At best, however, such 'laughing at the idiots' humour satiates the potential for resistance, while at worst it contributes to the obfuscation of political reality, ultimately feeding a divisive culture and making solidarity less possible.

Political comedians like John Oliver got a lot of flak from the media in these years. Writing for *Russia Today* in 2018, Michael McCaffrey called Oliver 'a charlatan who appears to be a rebellious liberal comedian speaking truth to power' but who is really 'a shameless shill for the ruling class in the US'. Seemingly radical tirades of mockery can be yet another brand of conformism, espousing the very values that are to blame for the current political crisis but presenting them as the solution to the problem. On the BBC in the same year, Slavoj Žižek also targeted Oliver, claiming that the 'half-joking' attitude of such presenters who patronizingly mock the ordinary people shows 'the ultimate failure of the Left'.

Both are necessary points, while at the same time each – along with thousands of Facebook pages over the period – turned to humorously target the ordinary liberal (embodied by Oliver and his viewers) in place of the elitist autocrat, structurally mimicking the humour that liberals used to take attack the Right. Though the target of the laughter has changed, satisfying those bored by ridiculing the Right and seeking a new target in the equally complicit liberal, the effect is much the same. The important political point here is that while capitalist liberalism must be as much the target of criticism as the Right, it cannot be targeted with exactly the same tactics. While the identarian content of right-wing politicians might be attacked by such jokes, the structural form of capitalism cannot. While political comedy is critical, this content-focused comedy can't be political in the truest sense of the word.

These years are also characterized by a fear of the power of comedy when it seemed to be deployed so affectively by the online Right. The problem was embodied in Poland when liberal-leftists Michał Maleszka and Mateusz Trzeciak criticized the modern 'culture of ironic distance and vulgar laughter', using the examples of 4chan and dank memes. Both claim that dank memes are a hermetic source of laughter, which creates distance between groups, thereby rejecting the ideas of solidarity and community that are crucial to organized resistance. One problem with their piece is that it is so pompous and devoid of humour itself that it offers no practical solution other than abstaining from all things funny. Another is that it inadvertently suggests abstention from the political by alienating everyday internet users from the political realm that their memes are attempting to infiltrate. This anxiety does, however, indicate that the humour of the progressive community was missing something that the humour of their enemies appeared to have in abundance. While the humour of progressives was failing to have political effect, it seemed humour was having political impact elsewhere.

A convincing critique of the patterns of humour prevalent among the online Left as well as among the liberals and right-wingers they criticize could be provided via French Marxist Henri Lefebvre. In his *Critique of Everyday Life* Lefebvre joined Marx's idea of alienation with comedy, using Chaplin as his prime case study. While appreciating Chaplin's potentially subversive comedy, Lefebvre concludes his discussion with the realization that 'on leaving the darkness of the cinema' after a Chaplin movie, 'we rediscover the same world as before, it closes round us again'. Since, 'the comic event has taken place, we feel decontaminated, returned to normality, purified somehow, and stronger'.

Lefebvre's work points to the problem of satiety in the kinds of comedy prevalent on social media during the period up until 2024. Such acts of comedy – themselves a symptom of the desperation of political progressives today, simulate a feeling of success and produce a sense of productivity and satisfaction without initiating any kind of political change. Proving the point, the UK Left expressed surprise that then-Prime Minister David Cameron could overcome 'Piggate' (in which it was claimed he had put his penis in a pig's mouth at The Bullingdon Club in Oxford) and that Hunt could retain political dignity after the Sousaphones, but the widespread online mockery and derision ultimately caused neither much trouble and indeed may have assisted them by satiating a desirous anger that might otherwise have ended up on the streets outside of Westminster.

Compared with the libidinal Right, who survive jokes as a matter of course, the Democrats present themselves as more serious. The Right have always been ripe for parody but have also long been highly skilled at avoiding the damage

SATIRE AND SATIATION FROM BREXIT TO TRUMP '24

it can cause. While Nigel Farage could overcome any humorous mockery imaginable (UKIP leaders were even known to eat the eggs thrown at them by protestors), Hillary Clinton could hardly have lasted after her shimmy and the dancing GIFs, even though Trump was more popular after meme-ably dancing to YMCA in 2016. The point here is an uncomfortable one. The libidinal Right is able to laugh at itself and, since this kind of comedy is the basis for solidarity and community, the Right is therefore coming out on top when it comes to recruiting support and creating movements of people.

Like Oliver, the more apparently progressive and mainstream community seems unable to achieve this. Another contemporary example of this kind of satirical comedy, which has characterized this period, would be British comedian Jonathan Pie, who got his first BBC show in 2018 and whose *Heroes and Villains* tour took place in 2024. Jonathan Pie is a strange act. It's comedy, but it has no jokes. It's satire, but there's no ironic gap between what the character says and the message we're meant to take from it. One half of the team behind the character – actor Tom Walker – has been criticized for taking

65

selfies with fascists at Tommy Robinson's Brexit march, while the other half – journalist Andrew Doyle – is implicated in revelations about *Spiked! Magazine*, which he edits, being revealed to have been funded by the Republican Koch Brothers Foundation.

But this is not quite the point. The greater concern in culture today may not be that entertainers, thinkers and politicians are 'secretly' fascist or sympathetic to the 'alt right'. Rather, the more important thing for the Left to be perceptive of, is the parts of right thinking that many centrists, liberals, and even left-wingers are privately perfectly comfortable with: and these tendencies are getting more marketable by the day. The BBC has, since at least 2010, responded to accusations of liberal bias by deliberately courting the populist right (Nigel Farage, well before UKIP's 2015 election success, made him a relevant voice) and even far-right (more recently, Tommy Robinson). While the BBC might claim – in classic 'free speech' manner – to have opened these voices up for criticism, it seems hard to argue that the BBC has not at the same time needlessly given credence and respectability to their views. If Farage and Robinson represented the BBC hearing the siren call of the right at the level of politics, we should be concerned that Pie represents a similar gesture at the level of culture. It might even be that Pie is brought on out of jealousy of the successful deployment of comedy on the Right and in an attempt to invite the audience to be in on the joke, while also telling them what to think.

The great satirist Jonathan Swift trusted that his readers would not approve of his proposal for eating the children of Irish peasants, but rather would recognize it as an exaggeration of the sort of heartless idea the kind of English aristocrat he was attacking might come up with. Another news-based satirist, Chris Morris's absurd headlines on *The Day Today* are delivered with deadpan seriousness, but the 'message' we receive is that news media itself is somehow absurd. When, by contrast, Pie rants to the camera against identity politics or tax avoidance, his targets are assumed to be those shared by the laughing participant. If there is any laughter at the terrible attempted humour, it relies on the ideological position of the viewer, who enjoys it and assumes they are correct in relation to a naive observer, who doesn't get it or is stupid enough to disagree.

In this way, it is a more prescriptive ideological comedy than its apparent predecessors, directing its viewer not only to be *against* something ridiculous and absurd but to be *for* something that it would be ridiculous or absurd to be against. His comedy might even share something of the logic of the far-right publication *Daily Stormer*'s style guide – in which Andrew Anglin gives potential contributors advice as to how to get racist views to gain traction among readers – and which reads, 'the unindoctrinated should not be able to tell if we are joking or not'. When it is designed to tell the viewer didactically exactly what to think, or simply to invite them to agree under the cover of comedy, satire is not what it used to be.

In finishing *Last Week Tonight* with a call to arms to his viewers, demanding the use of hashtags as political action, Oliver, like those worried about Pepe memes, knows something is missing in the comedy of the progressives. For Oliver, whether people use the hashtag or not marks the difference between active participation and active spectatorship. In reality, the more viral the use of the hashtag, the more satiated the group in question becomes and the less likely true participation and a genuine resistance is, particularly because its virality is most often a symptom of its circulation in one fixed portion of the internet rather than in universal spaces. In place of a desire to enact change is a simulated satisfaction. In this sense much satiating online humour may indeed be said to reveal the failure of today's political progressives, who have mastered the art of circulating didactic content within their bubbles and lost the ability to participate in the truly political act of a comedy that makes universalist solidarity possible.

Memes and Group Psychology

This parodic and endlessly repeated humour may do more than satiate feelings of discontent and discourage political activity. Memes may be something like the modern form of caricature, functioning to repeat the original so many times and in so many variations that the original itself is lost and a new reality comes into being. The end result of this process is the creation of aforementioned dank memes – so overused that they require another meme to be relevant again, which in turn leads to an accumulation of images that are meaningless on their own. But there is a redemptive humour possible, even in the most ideological attempts at humour, and at least at their peak moment memes were an important example of this.

Nineteenth-century artist Honoré Daumier – the father of modern caricature – anticipated the meme with his caricature set of Louis Philippe, published in Charles Philipon's *Le Caricature* in 1831. In that image he drew four caricatures of Philippe, each one increasingly resembling a pear. An image is repeated until the original can no longer be viewed except through the prism of the copy and Louis-Philippe – when we look back at the original – appears to have always already been a pear. A comparable near-contemporary example is Steve Bell's famous set of *Guardian* cartoons of David Cameron as a condom, which forever changed the connotations of his forehead for the UK population (though it did nothing to affect his vote count, nor did it prevent him returning to politics in 2023). As we've seen, these apparently progressive comic attacks seem to have no negative effect on their target and might even serve weirdly to enamour the public to them.

What might have been seen as a subversive gesture, taking down a politician or a monarch,

MEMES AND GROUP PSYCHOLOGY

seems to have just as much to do with building one up. Humour is not always about failure: it is an event that can go either way. This debate arose very interestingly in the context of Polish politics and political satire in the early Trump years. In separate articles, several liberal-leftist writers questioned the validity of the humour in the viral YouTube comedy series Ucho Prezesa, which caricatured the present Polish government. The premise of the show is that the hero of the series – based on Jarosław Kaczynski, the then leader of the populist Law and Justice party – runs the country from his office. The show was popular mostly among anti-government liberals, although even Kaczynski himself has reportedly spoken fondly of it. This is exactly the issue that both Grzegorz Rzeczkowski and Jakub Dymek have with the show. The show presents the cabinet ministers as harmless and not particularly smart, while Kaczynski is the intuitive mastermind, playing everyone like pawns from behind his desk. The series does criticize the party's leader as being ignorant, arrogant and backwards economically, but it also humanizes him to the point that viewers warm to him because of the portrayal. What is more, like Alex Baldwin's famous

71

impression of Trump, the Kaczynski from the show might actually soften the image of the president in the long term.

At the time of 2016, Trump seemed uncomfortable with those joking about him and would often fight back in speeches but, over the years, he seems to have noticed that this is less to his detriment than to his advantage. In the run up to the 2024 election, his own 'realdonaldtrump' Instagram, for instance, featured meme content about his opponents but also about himself and his own personality and its ability to lend itself to comedy. Such humour, he seems to realize, can help enamour the public to the subject of caricature. Caricature and meme may always play this function of building a group around a target, adding to the centrality and charm of it. In memed politics the reality is not only hidden but transformed. While there is a temptation to use ridicule to attack Trump, Le Pen, Cameron, Hunt and Kaczynski, they always weathered that approach, or even benefited from it.

Didactic intentional comedy works in particular because of its relationship to the patterns of digitization that have dominated corporate 'platform' capitalism over recent decades. What

MEMES AND GROUP PSYCHOLOGY

is commonly called a filter bubble has been variously theorized in media studies as the 'splinternet' or as cyberbalkanization, all words that speak to the function of social and digital media to create loops of self-reflective hyperlinks keeping its users in bubbles of users close to their own predicted or data-driven demographic. We now spend large portions of our time in online micro-economies of libidinal pleasure – each rife with humour in the form of shortform video content, jokes and memes – which speak only to those groups to whom the content is addressed, dividing us from each other and making a more universal solidarity less likely than ever. To cut a long story short, what ends up happening is the creation of a closed circuit of didactic humour in which only those designed to experience it do, leaving its potential as a political tool for activism almost redundant. Memes are now more organized by these curation techniques but, in the years of their peak political power, their virality was marked by being able to break out of these bubbles.

Since humour refuses to be purely didactic, and insists on universalizing, it cuts against these ideological attempts to deploy it in this oppositional way, even in the digital spaces that are inherent structures to support that type of information sharing. In a society desperate to use humour didactically to bolster oppositional politics, humour itself has other ideas. It is in its very failure that comedy finds its success and in its very successes that are found its failures.

Comedy points to the knot of subjectivity, so that when it works it doesn't and when it doesn't work it does. When it is able to create an ideology and inculcate its laughers into it, thereby being successful comedy, it remains as a dangerous signal of where that ideological position emerged from. Similarly, when it fails to establish its ideology, it fails as comedy; it leaves things unchallenged and unchanged, but can become true (accidental) comedy when it shows this failed attempt and its anxieties. In aligning themselves with didactic comedy, liberals set themselves up for this kind of failure, whereas it seems that the Right – perhaps unconsciously – has taken the caricaturists approach and embraces a more dynamic relationship between subject and comedy. Perhaps Trump can even be said to have cottoned on to the universalist core of humour, even where the rest of his politics fails.

A current example of a joke that circulated in social media and attempted to cross the divides of the filter bubbles – and point out the limits of this oppositional humour – is this critique of both the Conservative and Labour parties in current UK politics by British comedian Mark Jennings. The joke responds to the fact that there is less difference between the parties than ever before.

> To me the difference between Labour and the Tories is a bit like the difference between 'softbois' and 'fuckbois'. They're two kinds of guys that you get on dating apps, and neither of them actually cares about you, but they have got different tactics to try to win you over.
>
> Labour are 'softbois' because they pretend to be caring and considerate, saying things like 'Oh, I believe in equality', 'I'm a feminist too' and 'I do my bit for the environment', 'I'm not like those other guys.' Then you give them what they want and they say 'Look, I know I made all these promises but I'm just not looking for anything right now.'
>
> Tories are 'fuckbois' because they don't even try to pretend that they are not dicks, they just cut right to the chase and say 'Come on, just let me . . .',

'just let me . . .', 'just let me lower your taxes, come on', 'don't pretend like you don't want me to, no one even needs to find out.' Once you give them what they want, you never hear from them again until the next election. You get the text at 3 am and it says, 'you up?'

The joke works for two key reasons. First, it connects the politics of the present to the online world of contemporary slang around online dating and relationships. Positing the political party in the guise of a love object already asks us to confront our own libidinal relationship to our politics, and is already funny. Second, it points to the structure of the two ostensibly opposed political parties. While they seem similar, each leaves the subject equally unsatisfied. Each offers a different kind of lure, which promises pleasure in the moment, but has no intention of satisfying the subject in the long run. This can be understood in psychoanalytic terms as the way in which 'group psychology' invites the subject into a particular form of temporary pleasure, which involves the subject giving up what they themselves want to enjoy – the libidinal moment of the group.

MEMES AND GROUP PSYCHOLOGY

In his work on group psychology, in a section entitled 'Suggestion and Libido' Freud seems almost to talk to the digital libidinal economy of memes, curated shortform humour reels and demographically targeted suggestions and adverts of the present moment. It is here that he argues that there is a particular form of pleasure found not in following one's desires but in giving up what one desires for the collective desires of the group. This is not a selfless giving up of individualistic pleasure for a greater good but a function of pleasure in general: we are invited to enjoy the desire of the group in place of our own desires. Croatian philosopher Srećko Horvat has discussed the nature of Barrack Obama's 'yes, we can' campaign in almost these terms, as an invitation to insert oneself into the desire of a group, but it was probably Trump who deployed it most effectively with statements like 'build the wall', which have less to do with responding to the people's desire for a wall and more to do with inviting them to replace their individual desires with those of the group. Meme communities that coalesced around Trump did this with skill and subtlety, often using post-irony and humour to galvanize a community, not by responding to their desires but by inviting them to participate in the collective desire of the community.

Also advocating for a new focus on Freud's work on group psychology in *Freud and the Limits of Bourgeois Individualism*, Léon Rozitchner argues for an urgent return to Freud's work on group psychology. He argues that:

> Just as Claude Lévi-Strauss used to say about every new marriage that it actualized all the others and brushed up against incest by actualizing the repressive pact, the same could be said about every group or mass in which the contradictions once again become condensed around a repressive scheme: they brush up against the previous revolution from which they necessarily derive, and actualize as an ambiguous moment the transition from nature to culture, from the primal horde to the fraternal alliance. (2023, 487)

In the same way that for Lévi-Strauss marriage touches upon a primary incest taboo by approaching it to protect against it, we might say that comedy touches upon a primary anxiety by approaching it to move away from it. In the contemporary political situation it is more important to see this in terms of group psychology, as Freud did, than ever before. The move of comedy takes us from our universal anxiety to the safety of group thinking, in which that anxiety is approached precisely to be dealt with and denied. It transitions us from nature (universal lack) to culture (oppositional security). As Rozitchner puts it, the contradictions of subjectivity are condensed around a repressive scheme. In this sense, group psychology is not about giving up the narcissism of the self in favour of being more open to others but rather about denying our universal connections and contradictions in favour of closing off others in oppositional conclusive thinking. On the contrary, to the typical didactic humour of the moment, which works in exactly this way, Jennings's joke confronts us with the promise of group psychology and shows us that we are all – universally – invited into it.

Keks and LOLs: Playground Humour

In 2023, some UK schools sent out a text to parents saying that any student found supporting Andrew Tate would be placed into isolation and made subject to investigation. From the left–liberal perspective, supporting Andrew Tate (rather than, say, Greta Thunberg) is tantamount to rationally sympathizing with child traffickers and 'fascist' alpha males from the misogynist past. From the perspective of the kek-chanting image-board provocateurs of the online right, it is less about politics (with a capital P) than it is about inflammatory play. The idea of kek originated from a translation from the Korean version of LOL and developed into a symbol for the online Right of Pepe memes and image boards, even producing ideas like the fictional nation of Kekistan and the Cult of Kek, both of which contained white supremacist material in parts of the community. At the level of content, these communities and their jokes contained racist and impermissible content.

Nevertheless, at the level of form, they utilized a humour and a play that progressives were lacking. In many cases, rather than rationally motivated political statements with concrete (racist or supremacist, for instance) aims, they were libidinally motivated transgressions designed 'for the LOLs', as the slogan of the time went. These acts might be instinctively political, but they are not 'right-wing' or 'fascist' until they become so. If fascism is seen as a content, these eruptions were often guilty of it, but if fascism is seen as a form they were far from it. Instinctive and provocative political play can become dangerous, but it can also become emancipatory or subversive.

An attention-seeking teenager blurting out his support for Tate under a muffled cough in his science class is an instinctive attempt to reveal the police-like rules of the secondary-school classroom (Foucault and his memes were right after all). It is precisely the possibility that an official school text could go out to parents banning the act that engenders the desire to commit it in the first place. At a stretch, a line can be drawn (at the level of content) between these acts and those of the online Right, as the teachers of the Tate-coughing student feared, but one does not lead to the other. Transgressive play, in its form, is political and community forming, and a culture of fear that polices it too quickly because of its content risks allowing it only to belong to the toxic communities that this policing attempts to prevent. By regulating spaces (from an early age), the idea is to press out violent and dangerous thinking and set the precedent for a less tainted future, thus banishing fascism and violence from the system. At the same time, it becomes increasingly clear that more regulation only leads to more radicalization and to more desire to provoke.

A provocative tweet sent into the ether anticipates the response of the Other, which arrives as a form of validation even and especially when it vehemently denounces the act itself. For every tweet that gets in trouble, there are a thousand more that fail to (a clear example of the perverse *subject-supposed-to-No!*, discussed in the next section). The school's threat to 'isolate' Tate supporters is not dissimilar to the online tactics of individuals, and the institutions of social media, who report, block and isolate transgressive tweeters with unpalatable opinions. This doubling of alienation intensifies the desire of those users to commit acts with this potential effect. Of course, it is precisely the outcome that hegemonic political actors of the moment want, since they rely on these transgressors to sustain the 'look how bad it would be without us' position that has become the go-to of contemporary political centrism.

There has been something of a reversal of roles, since the ability to refuse regulation and to romantically embrace transgression has historically been much celebrated by liberal culture. During the riots of May '68, still heralded as a symbol for the Left by many, one of the most popular slogans was 'jouir sans entraves' – enjoy without limits. It was then considered positively radical to be unregulated at the level of culture and its norms, even if it was the logic of capitalism to be unregulated at the level of economics. Now, it is deemed best to be perfectly regulated – correct – at the level of culture (illustrated in the idea of searching for impure tweets in this archive of your enemies), while it remains capitalist to spend with freedom. *Yes we can* (to borrow Obama's phrase) has become *no you can't*, but capitalism continues apace.

The 'culture wars' embody a mystification of material reality by obscuring things into simple oppositions. Couching things in oppositional terms – Tate vs Thunberg, the monarchy vs Harry and Meghan, AOC vs Trump – they set up a moralistic and didactic sense of ethics that characterizes our contemporary moment. This forces us into established positions within a system – both of which are required to keep that system going. Careers are built on being anti-fascist, so they require the fascist to keep going, just as cops are built on the existence of robbers and shopkeepers on the existence of customers. Fascists vs Antifa has no doubt featured in playgrounds before now.

Play involves learning these rules but also potentially breaking them: a provocative, politics in science class, etc. While the trend in thinking around education and radicalization seems to want to reach back into childhood and implement their rules there to eradicate the threat of bad behaviour later down the line, it fails to see that eruptions of violent transgression against their cultural codes are rooted in the fact that there is not enough play, rather than that there is too much.

The psychoanalyst Nicholas Abraham coined the concept of 'anasemia'. Anasemia refers to a transformation of meaning that happens when 'the same old words' appear in a new context, when a flash of understanding takes place that can be thought of as interpretation, while at the same time transformative of our reality. Psychoanalysis itself functions anasemically. For example, when we learn a concept (such as that of 'the unconscious') we understand ourselves differently and subjectivity shifts because of the interpretive moment where a new visibility is possible.

If the word anasemia appears to suggest amnesia, it may be because an anasemic event cannot be unseen, to the point where it is impossible to access the past once it has taken place. Once we learn a few psychoanalytic concepts, we can't look at our psychotic husbands or hysterical wives in the same way. In general discourse, a word like autism would be a good example of how anasemia can function – it is an interpretation of symptoms, which also transforms the culture and makes it impossible to go back. It may be socially or culturally useful or it may be harmful and destructive, but it certainly changes things.

Memes, perhaps, are the ultimate anasemic cultural phenomena. A meme is an interpretation that transgresses the limits of a situation to reveal its limitations. It is a kind of play that breaks the rules, not in order to prove them but to move on from them. While the tweets of the provocateur simply serve to give the rule-makers of mainstream culture what they want, these acts restructure the situation itself via interpretation. True play is re-interpretation in precisely this anasemic sense and comedy is perhaps the ultimate form of adult anasemia. The joke cannot be unmade, and it places existing words and concepts in a new position and allows us to explore and experiment with our relationship as subjects to our ideology and our social life. The natural space for these jokes is the playground, which operates as a 'commons' from which social life is built, and some concessions might need to be made at the level of content to allow it to preserve this.

With didactic moralism policing play further and further back into childhood, we risk a future society that has not worked out how to live by – and influence – its own rules. We could even say that the policing of play – and of humour – is the symptom of a repressive society that is most likely to produce the kind of oppositional thinking that leads to fascism, transphobia, racism and homophobia, the very things that the policing claims to combat. Capitalism, of course, wants us to take the sides of free speech or discourse policing and sustain this self-fulfilling system. Capitalism requires the contingent obstacle (Andrew Tate for one side, 'woke' police for the other) to function in order to sustain its fantasy and to distract from the fact that the system itself is the cause of our problems.

Milk Pouring and Trolling: Perverse, Psychotic, Neurotic

The policing of playgrounds is connected to the history of the internet. In the mid 1990s when the internet became a household thing, the social sides of online communities were dominated by AOL and MSN Messenger, chat rooms and forums. The main activity in these spaces was piss taking: ribbing, criticizing, attacking, often brutally and seriously. Today, much of this activity would be labelled as trolling. Much of it would be reported and even censored in advance.

In 2009, Mark Zuckerberg gave a speech in which he famously stated: 'you have one identity'. As the media theorist José van Dijk has shown, the logic marked a turning point in the history of social media. From this point on, catfishing and fake accounts becomes a thing, and so does trolling. Before that, the concepts didn't exist, not because the behavior did not exist but because it was not identified as abnormal or unique. Before 2009, the idea of messing about in what was really an online playground, full of anonymity and openness, dominated conceptions of the internet. Sherry Turkle's famous article 'Who Am We?' from 1996 embodied this multiple identity heart of the digital space: it was a space of play for gender, sexuality, morality and ethics in which users were multiple and anonymous.

We might say that trolling is traumatic only to a particular form of identity – the dominant form of identity today, which has its roots in this post-2009 social media. This form of identity is no doubt a particularly capitalist one. It may be no coincidence that the identity-focused social media of post 2009 emerges right on the back of the economic crisis of 2008. The gesture seems to be that in place of economic security we are offered protected identities. Further, the unifying of online accounts into singular identities is of course a process designed to turn each (economically precarious) subject into a commodity of which they are responsible for the self-care.

Further, it promises the commoditized subject a recognition under platform capitalism that, structurally, cannot be fulfilled. If the American of the early twentieth century was, for Steinbeck, a temporarily frustrated millionaire, the online subject of the early twenty-first century may be a temporarily frustrated 'influencer'. The unified subject of social media presents the promise to the user that the widely recognized influencer is an emergent of this new economic model. From a Marxist perspective, it is not the unrecognized user who is the mistake that proves the rule of recognition under the regime of platform capitalism, but rather the influencer themself that masks the flaws in the system — the glitch that proves the rule of non-recognition.

That glitch is the target of the troll, and one particularly interesting series of examples of trolling and comedy from recent years shows us the different forms of antagonist humour and their policing, which are prominent in our online social lives: those surrounding milk. There is a more than a fortuitous or coincidental connection between trolling and milk, which helps us explore our visceral reactions to others and the role of comedy in these exchanges.

Psychoanalytically speaking, we should say that milk has a history of being connected to ideas of attraction and repulsion: milk is often found particularly repulsive and is a common fear or phobia, as well as being the symbol of fulfilment and wellbeing. From Hitchcock's use of Bates carrying a glass of milk upstairs in *Psycho* to the infamous milk bar in Kubrick's *A Clockwork Orange,* there is always something frightening about this childhood object of desire.

Melanie Klein's psychoanalytic work on the cycle of deprivation in the breast routine is the most important theorization of our relationship to milk. For Klein, the breast (and its milk) become both good and bad (which she calls 'the good breast' and 'the bad breast') because the child comes to a love–hate relationship with the parents via the regulation of their access to milk. In her famous formulation 'they deprive me because I hate them, I hate them because they deprive me', the child comes to develop this ambivalent attraction/repulsion approach to people and things with the milk as the primary object which sets this contradiction in motion.

The less well-known psychoanalyst August Starcke placed the origins of castration in the breast. For him, the father taking away the baby from the mother's breast operated as a 'precastration' in the removal of the penis-like milk vessel from the child, which had formerly seen that vessel as a part of itself. Whether we agree entirely with these childhood-based interpretations, there is a critical reminder in milk of a childhood attraction/repulsion dynamic. This is a universal condition – we all drank the milk, whatever creed, gender or race we might belong to – so the milk may have a certain universalism in taking us back to fundamental formational moments in the history of our subjectifies.

Trolling is also about attraction and repulsion. We are tempted in by it and we are repelled by it. Originally, the targets of trolling were celebrities or those with large online followings. On infamous trolling sites like kiwifarms and lolcow, the logic of the trolling was always to bring down an apparently undivided image of a subject (the celebrity) to the material level of the vulnerable and divided human subject. Of course, certain forms of trolling cross into illegal and dangerous practices, but the policing of trolling per se might be a symptom of the fact that we need more than ever to protect the appearance of our identities (connected to our increasing economic precarity) and we can less than ever bear to confront our universal human subjectivity. This may be why milk – with its regressive castrating implications – seemed to be such an effective, and funny, trolling technique in the 2020s.

Some milk activism is perverse. The right-wing activist Baked Alaska was maced by unknown assailants during a rally and a video that showed him pouring milk on his face to try to neutralize the chemical went viral. The milk was then ironically reclaimed and turned into a symbol for the 'Pepe' meme-sharing crowd of ironic Trump supporting online activists. Self-proclaimed white supremacist Richard Spencer, for instance, started using the milk emoji, which eventually led to the 'cows are racist' trolling movement that attempted to poke the sensibility of liberals prone to accusing everything they don't like of being racist.

The now-notorious liberal art project of 2017 'He Will Not Divide Us' (created by Luke Turner and – probably disingenuously on the part of the artist – deploying the fame of Shia Laboeuf) was humorously trolled by online activists from the 'alt-Right' (as was the *nom du jour*). The event was a self-conscious purity project, in which a camera was set up to run 24/7 and participants were invited to constantly chant the slogan 'he will not divide us' on repeat. Right-wing 'trolls' attended the space in Brooklyn and broke all the rules, which were indeed quite strict, by pouring

MILK POURING AND TROLLING

milk over their heads, making dog-whistle comments to image-board communities and baiting 'honest' participants into embarrassing acts of violence and aggression. They perhaps deserved to be sent home with a red note, like the teenager coughing Andrew Tate support. They were, of course, labelled as criminal fascists.

Psychoanalytically, we can say that to drink this milk the participant needs to act as an uncastrated subject. This can be thought of as perversion, defined in Lacanian thinking as the disavowal of castration. The pervert acts specifically out of the illusion of their jouissance being the jouissance of the Other. The dick pic is a good example of this perverse idea of desire: I assume you want this, and even if you don't, your desire is framed in relation to mine. Perhaps we can say that these milk-pouring Pepe fans are asking to be castrated and reaching out to the Other to be told off in a world of absent father figures. In her book on perversion Stephanie Swales argues for 'the subject-supposed-to-No!', examining a subject named Ray, who expresses a deep desire to be told off and replace the absent father (Swales 2012, 243). The appeal of Donald Trump might be seen in this perverse light, as might the acts of the milk chugging online activists at the Brooklyn art exhibit. While they seem to be acting as uncastrated 'macho' American alphas, there is at heart a desire to be brought into a universally castrated social world.

Not all the milk pourers are perverse. Some might be more psychotic. It might even be that far more intent on denying their castration than the 'alt-Right' activists chugging the milk are the Vegan activists pouring milk all over the floor of Selfridges. Done to raise awareness of the environmental impact of the dairy industry, the confident viral act seems more uncastrated than even the chuggers.

These subjects are psychotic in the Lacanian schema. To understand psychosis in Lacanian terms it is necessary to see the difference between repression and foreclosure. Through the process of repression, an element of signification is cast to the unconscious, where it continues to threaten the conscious subject. On the other hand, through foreclosure, something is rejected from the symbolic entirely, with no hope of return. Then, the subject indulges in more and more deeply held fantasies, which appear to speak to this irreparable hole, not in the subject

MILK POURING AND TROLLING

themselves but in external reality. Lacan writes that 'in psychosis, reality itself initially contains a hole that the world of fantasy will subsequently fill' (Lacan 1997, 45).

Vegan milk pouring might be seen as the ultimate psychotic expression of denying the universal nature of trauma. By framing the vegans as the pure subject and the meat eaters at Selfridges or at Salt Bae's elite restaurants as the guilty and complicit other, they psychologically deny the nature of the divided subject – the recognition of which is the possibility for politics and social change. Whether they conceive of the milk-drinkers as the feral uncastrated other in need of castration (perhaps as they admit themselves) or themselves as the pure undivided true subject, they believe that there are differences between us.

But what makes both of these milk pourers so viral and draws our attention to them so forcefully, which is why the activist act works, is its weird and almost uncanny humour. Although the milk pouring is a psychical act, it can be better understood as a digital one since it works by anticipating virality and online circulation, much like the Russian anti-Police memes. The psychical encounter becomes a digital one. We can say that the Other of the social media encounter is undivided, in both their successes and their failures and therefore, in the eyes of the subject, cannot provide them with the recognition that would usually occur in the intersubjective encounter. Likewise, both sets of milk pourers – consciously speaking – attempt to present the undivided subject in relation to the weakness of the Other. But the humorous excess of the milk works against this logic.

The comedy of the milk forces us into a neurotic realization. In Lacanian terms, neuroticism is considered the normal process for the development of a subject. When this development goes wrong, the psychotic or pervert emerges through a failure to deal with the reality of the impossibility of total satisfaction of desire. The neurotic is repressed: they deny the awareness of castration, and the lack in the Other and in themselves, but they bury their lack not in the external world but in their own unconscious. Though repressed, there is lack just underneath the surface of the subject. The neurotic subject is split between physical, pre-linguistic, instinctual urges, and symbolic, linguistic, abstract constraints as imposed by their castration and repression in the

MILK POURING AND TROLLING

world of language. They are in this sense consistently confronting and turning away from their lack as a subject.

Milk, strewn across the floor of Selfridges or flowing over the lips and chin of a troll at an art project, reminds us of this primary castration and of our divided nature as subjects neurotically held in this dialectical relationship to ourselves. It does so not just because it is milk – which is capable of being funny or uncanny – but because it is employed precisely in an attempt to divide us. The comedy, and the virality, of the milk shows that it does not do so, and that it insists on uniting us instead, reaching out of its intended audience and uniting us in laughter. Those who take it too seriously – such as Piers Morgan ranting about the vegan milk pourers on TalkTV or Shia LaBeouf panicking about the Trump activists at his art exhibit – treat it with perversion or psychosis. Those of us who laugh together, and experience the universalist reminder of the milk, neurotically create social and political possibilities together.

Activist or Fetishist

One interesting effect of the replacement of the laughter of solidarity with the laughter of didacticism is the retreat of laughter from activist protests and demonstrations. When the Society of Blue Buckets protests took over the streets of Russia in 2010, there was a meme-like humour at the heart of activism. Protestors placed blue buckets on their car roofs to mimic the blue lights of the emergency services, and soon cyclists copied with buckets on their helmets, and protestors attached small blue buckets to their dogs, partly in order to go viral on the internet through the memetic humour of the gesture. In a classic example of this form of humour, anti-Putin protestors of 2010 at Bolotnaya Ploshchad's demonstrations used phrases like 'Bring Back Fair Elections' next to other placards displaying nonsense like 'Bring Back Snowy Winters'. As Olga Goriunova has shown, this pre-history of meme anticipates virality by attaching humour to activism and perhaps – most importantly – by humanizing and universalizing the experience.

Conflicts – and our responses to them – raise the question of our libidinal relationship to crisis:

do passionate performances like those of the anti-war movement that lobbied against the Vietnam War, or even against invasions of Afghanistan and Iraq in the early 2000s, still serve their purpose in a time of side-taking flag waving: Russia versus Ukraine, Israel versus Palestine? This rise of the flags as symbols of gestural sympathy, from Facebook doling out national flags as filters for profile pictures after terrorist attacks in affected countries (the French flag after Charlie Hebdo, the Belgian flag, the US flag, etc.) results in its take-up by corporations and governments: as in the mass display of the Ukrainian flag. Many states pre-emptively flew Ukraine's flag, in sympathy, and supposed solidarity, with an attacked nation; they also flew Israel's flag, after October 7th – and this to likewise control the narrative. Yet, in picking up what they perceive to be the flag of the oppressed to combat these official narratives, activists buy into the logic of the system itself.

While at moments like this we often hear people accused of fetishizing their objects of empathy, the real problem is that activism is not properly fetishistic enough. The crisis shows the Left's redundancy in the face of crisis, when it has become unable to do anything but champion purist ethical subjects over apparently uncomplicated dastardly enemies without recognizing its own libidinal investment in the matter.

Much has been said of the role of desire in activism, especially since 2008, when Obama's 'Yes, we can' campaign used new digital tools to foster a community desire to get behind one candidate, with unexpected results. Following that were the Trump election and Brexit, which made the same desire-oriented canvassing tactics more visible. Because they were now in the hands of the Chan bros and British nationalists (the wrong people in the eyes of the commentariat) they were criticized and even criminalized, ultimately resulting in the Cambridge Analytica scandal and the obsession with the concept of fake news and media manipulation. The message was that perhaps we shouldn't be following our desires after all, because they were being nefariously harnessed by those seeking to use them for ill. When it came to memes, the fear around the influence of things like Pepe the Frog was nothing short of hysterical. A kind of McCarthyism developed, in which humour, the liberals argued, was the dangerous cancer spreading virally through society and convincing us of all the wrong things.

That moment, perhaps merely fortuitously, might signal the eventual end of the ideas of May 1968 and its 'live without death', 'enjoy without limits' injunction to follow one's desires, which at the time was seen as subversive and revolutionary but which has seemingly come to an end. This leaves us in a different phase when it comes to the relationship between politics and desire. Are we to leave our desires out of it, which would likely be impossible anyway, when making political choices or statements? Or are we to trust our own desire, even if we deeply distrust those of others?

One criticism of the activists that we are likely to encounter is that they are guilty of fetishization. A paraphrase of what this criticism means is that they are guilty of putting too much of their own desire into their politics, using it to plug a gap in themselves rather than because they are rationally or logically committed to the *cause du jour*. Ukrainian flags on profile pictures or BLM pin badges might be a case in point of this apparently fetishist activism, and Palestinian flag art is the latest incantation. No doubt even in the most well-meaning support and shows of solidarity, an element of fetishism is present, or at least it appears to be. But this is not fetishist in the psychoanalytic sense of the word.

Of fetishism, Freud wrote that at one and the same time the fetishist is able to believe in his phantasy and to recognize that it is nothing but a phantasy. And yet, the fact of recognizing the phantasy as phantasy in no way reduces its power over the individual. The fetishist desires, but they understand their desire to be in the realm of fantasy, with no possible ultimate solution in the real material world.

In an interesting case in the Middle-East conflict, there are those who cannot see the role of their own fantasy in their activism. For pro-Israeli advocates, the terrorist subject of Hamas – real as it is – operates as the object that sustains the logic of its own identity and believes that eradicating this Other would close the gap in its desire and lead into the solution of the future. On the other hand, for some of those activists campaigning for Palestine, there is an uncritical investment in ideas of liberation and of the free subject and perhaps even a tendency to orientalize the subject by repressing the existence of swathes of antisemitism in the Middle East because it doesn't tally well with the subject-supposed-to-be-supported.

Where there is both extreme antisemitism and anti-Islamophobia, as well as the idealization and orientalizing of both the supposedly pure Palestinian subject and of the authentic Jewish right to land, there is an impasse. This impasse can only be overcome by the logic of the fetishist.

Comparisons between the peace process in Northern Ireland are obvious, and they might be a stretch too far. But what we can say is that in Northern Ireland a situation was eventually arrived at in which both sides could experience recognition. Despite decades of embedded (and continuing) hatred, a path was found that at least allowed the Other to be recognized and therefore to live. Like a fetishist, they recognize themselves and the Other as a subject of fantasy.

This universalist awareness of the fetishist – that we are all subjects caught in a fantasy of desire, whether Capitol-storming Trump supporter or pro-Palestine activist – is what is needed for the activist today. An impasse like that of our divided political world can only be broken by recognizing the Other, and by the implication of our (and their) desires in our political movements. We can't trust our desires like the '68-ers did, but we can recognize that we are all subjects of fantasy in our politics, even those on the other side. To recognize this is not the universalism of 'all lives matter', but the opposite: a universalism of lack in which what we universally share is our failure.

The Belfast comedian Vittorio Angelone is a case-in-point, and his humour is often divisive, though his recent joke can be taken in two ways:

> I have an English friend who is very very pro-Israel, and he was saying to me 'Vittorio, you don't understand what is going on over there. The Palestinians have elected terrorists to their government.' And I was like, 'What, I thought that was our thing?'

Like his jokes about the history of Northern Ireland, it might be designed to validate the right position over the wrong one, just as Acaster's humour does. These jokes invite the laughing subjects to see themselves as being on the right side of history by aligning one (perceived to be) inevitable position with one disputable one. Such humour would be like the joke about Brexiteers, it works only by creating an imagined idiot who would think otherwise to those laughing. In

ACTIVIST OR FETISHIST

February of 2024, Soho Theatre London had to apologize after comedian Paul Currie was antisemitic to a heckler who didn't want to applaud a Palestine flag. The heckler was eventually ejected from the theatre. Laughing – in activist terms – is often about affirming those who agree with us.

On the other hand, the joke may be read as universalist. Since the mainstream parties in Northern Ireland used to be either Republican or Loyalist militias, the 'universalist' point of the joke may after all be that all politicians are terrorists if you're going to go back far enough. In that sense, it is fetishist rather than activist, since it locates the subject's libidinal position in relation to ideology and forces them to be aware of it, rather than allowing the joke to fall only on the imperfections of the target.

The best joke of the brilliant American comedian Norm Macdonald, who died in 2021, leaves us with the sense of recognizing our own fantasy that the fetishist possesses and the activist lacks:

> A moth goes into a podiatrist's office, and the podiatrist's office says, 'What seems to be the problem, moth?'

ACTIVIST OR FETISHIST

The moth says 'What's the problem? Where do I begin, man? I go to work for Gregory Illinivich, and all day long I work. Honestly doc, I don't even know what I'm doing anymore. I don't even know if Gregory Illinivich knows. He only knows that he has power over me, and that seems to bring him happiness. But I don't know, I wake up in a malaise, and I walk here and there . . . at night I . . . I sometimes wake up and I turn to some old lady in my bed that's on my arm. A lady that I once loved, doc. I don't know where to turn to. My youngest, Alexendria, she fell in the . . . in the cold of last year. The cold took her down, as it did many of us. And my other boy, and this is the hardest pill to swallow, doc. My other boy, Gregarro Ivinalititavitch . . . I no longer love him. As much as it pains me to say, when I look in his eyes, all I see is the same cowardice that I . . . that I catch when I take a glimpse of my own face in the mirror. If only I wasn't such a coward, then perhaps . . . perhaps I could bring myself to reach over to that cocked and loaded gun that lays on the bedside behind me and end this hellish facade once and for all . . . Doc, sometimes I feel like a spider, even though I'm a moth, just barely hanging on to my web with an everlasting fire underneath me. I'm not feeling

ACTIVIST OR FETISHIST

good. And so the doctor says, 'Moth, man, you're troubled. But you should be seeing a psychiatrist. Why on earth did you come here?'

And the moth says, ''Cause the light was on.'

The joke turns on the naive observer mistaking the podiatrist for the psychiatrist and, as the moth goes on and on, the punchline becomes more anticipated. The Kafkaesque narrative, which like many long 'timewaster' jokes works by mocking the form of the joke, and even the recipient for listening for so long, set the scene for the punchline. That punchline shows that the whole history of literature and education can do nothing to mitigate against the moth's instinct to fly towards the light. One reading, and probably Macdonald's sense of the joke, would be that even the most literary culture and wizened lived experience pales in comparison with the forces of nature. But what makes the joke funny is that we all fly towards the light because we are subjects, and no amount of individual storytelling and lived experience can take us away from this fact of subjectivity. Like the moths going towards the light which destroys them, we are all divided subjects. The joke does what the fetishist is able to do – to recognize themselves and the Other as a subject of fantasy – but what the activist cannot.

Dancing Laughter and Clowns from St Vitus to TikTok

Since the dominance of social media, perhaps with the Korean popstar Psy's 2012 'Gangnam Style' as the opening gambit, comic dancing has been a consistent theme in contemporary humour, from Twerking to TikTok routines. Perhaps the infectious Harlem Shake of 2013 is the best example. It has reminiscences of the St Vitus dance, a name given to bouts of mania involving infectious erratic dancing, occurrences of which were reported from the fourteenth to seventeenth centuries. The phenomenon is sometimes called 'choreomania', from the Greek *choros*, meaning dance, and *mania*, meaning madness. The mania involves being taken over by (usually) temporary madness, sometimes in large groups and has been depicted by artists including both Breugel the Elder and Younger.

These moments no doubt connect to our cultural sense of order and disorder. Writing about

Hegel, Bertolt Brecht made a remarkable comment about Hegel's own philosophy in relation to the idea of choreomania.

> [Hegel] had what it takes to be one of the greatest comedians among philosophers, comparable only to Socrates, who had a similar method . . . He had a twitch of the eye, as far as I can see, with which he was born, like a birth defect and which he kept until his death, without him ever becoming conscious of it. He was always winking in the same way that others had an unsuppressable St Vitus dance. His sense of humour was such that he could not think, for example, of order without disorder. It was clear to him that in the immediate proximity of the greatest order, there was to be found the greatest disorder, and he even went so far as saying: in one and the same place! (Thanks to Mladen Dolar for this reference)

Brecht sees the logic of Hegel's thinking as being like that of the St Vitus dance because it has a comic logic that puts order and disorder together in the same place. The subject is born out of contradiction and, because of this, it can never truly be complete, pure or rational. We are created as failed, divided subjects with lack at our very core and, try as we might to impose completeness and order in our lives, the reminder of our origin always persists.

Comedy – as we've seen through this book – forms order out of disorder, sense out of anxiety and ideology out of language. However, it also shows this process coming into being – like the dancers of the St Vitus dance, signalling the disorder that persists. This is a distinctly Hegelian, and a distinctly comic, way of seeing the world, which embraces the void of existence. It is also a profoundly anticapitalist way of seeing the world, which we are encouraged increasingly to repress, hence the attack on comedy in contemporary society.

The aspiration to fill the void of existence is a utopian fantasy, which denies this fact, and it is one that capitalism sells to us as its core fantasy. To dwell within the productivity of that void is to shift one's libido from an infinite forward impulse – one that is dissatisfying because it never meets the subject's goals – to a circular infinity that foregrounds the enjoyment made possible by the void itself. In other words, it changes the subject's experience of dissatisfaction

– always feeling an apparently contingent loss in the object's failure to fulfil them – to an appreciation of the fundamental Lack that makes their subjectivity and desire possible.

In Todd Phillip's film *Joker* (2019), Arthur Fleck cannot confront the tragedy of his life and the miserable material conditions of the society of which he is part. He has waking dreams about a relationship with Sophie, an attractive woman who lives on his floor and a woman who, in reality, would never forge a relationship with a man like him.

The human tendency to invest religiously in the possibility of assuaging our lack via totality is so powerful that we would die for it. Not only can we come face to face with homelessness or the broadcast of war crimes on social media and yet still disavow the truth in our system, we can keep alive the logic of possibility not only in our own world, but in all others we imagine to be possible. We need to overcome the belief in the possibility of transcendence in all possible worlds, even those that exist in our imagination.

The context for the film is the capitalist system in which we compete for recognition that can only go to a few subjects. The Hollywood Star

System presented an impossible world of deified glamour out of reach of the average subject, who understood the prospects of their life to be without the scope of the reality of the movies. In contrast to this conservative, or 'feudal' approach, contemporary culture favours an ideology of representation, or the foregrounding of stars who are compelling because of their perceived normality, or in whom audiences invest because of their commodified lack. Now, the world of digital media – with its likes, shares and loops of recognition – steps into this role. This capitalist regime sells a possible world to the aspirant, in which they can imagine they might become a star, which leads to greater exploitation and the extraction of surplus value, when statistically – for the vast majority of aspirants – that world is impossible.

In terms of *Joker's* manifest content, Arthur can be understood as the sinthome of the 1980s, recession-era Gotham City in which he lives. The 'sinthome', a concept developed by Lacan, is the symptom that ties or sutures reality together. If its stitches are unpicked, the whole system of the subject unravels. It is the seam revealing the disorder in the system of order and, like Hegel's philosophy or the St Vitus dance, it makes its presence felt. Arthur's neurological disorder – manifested in laughing fits, the gruesome antithesis to the tragedy of his life – erupts when social services fail him, he loses his job and cannot afford medication. This sinthome (saintly man) bears the message of what is missing for him within Arthur's world: under a capitalist sky, he is alienated, individualized, impoverished and his condition exploited for laughs. His sinthome are the tics and grimaces of this society and those who are also disposed to identify so strongly with Arthur that they take to the streets in mass protests, masked according to the clown-like paint that marks Arthur's face. This eruption represents potentiality within the system, which – if directed towards the universal truth of the impossibility of the social structure – could become an emancipatory one.

On a micro level, laughter and humour can play this emancipatory role, even in a society that seems dedicated, and desperate, to relegate it to the level of didacticism. It can be a universalist, instinctive protest, which speaks to the possibility of society and therefore of revolution. With the humour of scripted TikTok routines and the viral twerks of a moment – though we might want to dismiss them as ridiculous – we see something like an approach to a collective spirit of St Vitus, a rare moment that attempts to speak universally at least to the possibility of an anti-capitalist acceptance of the void of existence. These moments are short-circuits in our libidinal investment in capitalism and they make another world possible. At the same time, through systems of commoditization, these moments are themselves turned back into the capitalist fantasy of fulfilment through fame and recognition, on the platforms through which they go viral. In this contradiction the essence of comedy is found.

Conclusion: Jokes, Masters and Orgasms

Contradiction cannot be commoditized insofar as it cannot offer absolution to the lack at the heart of subjectivity. This is the precise reason we are most shielded from it within capitalism; a tragedy, given how an orientation towards it could transform the way we live in the world. Capitalism is an exploitation of the religious tendency in subjectivity: the drive to seek oneness in oblivion and in the endless pursuit of commodities (though it offers none of the absolution that confessional religion provides). But capitalism may be collapsing into its new manifestation. The morbid symptoms of its crisis could confront us with the nature of our world and subjectivity and lead us, via collective politics, to an emancipatory future. Comedy points to the possibility of an intersubjective collective politics by confronting us with our subjectivity in a way that capitalism denies. Capitalism then, has to shield us from comedy.

Under the pervasive constraints of oppositional capitalist ideology, even philosophy, politics and art have become commodities. Art, film and philosophy have been drawn under the regime of neoliberal institutions where, instead of speaking and thinking freely, we neuter our insights in favour of a set of oppositional ideas that appear aesthetically to be thoughtful but do little other than sustain the extraction of surplus value and the generation of scapegoats – enemies – around whom the non-dialectical society rationalizes its own purity as it collapses around us. Comedy refuses to become a mere commodity and it refuses to keep us divided but, as with everything else in recent years, the conditions of capitalism have tried harder and harder to push it into the didactic fragments of self-affirming divisive discourse that much comedy has become.

Fernando León de Aranoa's 2021 comedy *The Good Boss* explores the changes in the history of comedy and capitalism as a shared history. It tells the story through a week in the life of a factory boss, played by Javier Bardem. Bardem's character begins the week revered as a traditional conservative boss, a figure of pure patriarchal order. By midweek he has become the failed figure of the master that serves contemporary liberal order, a boss whose castration ushers in a new era and allows others into power. Ultimately, the film shows us that this change from uncastrated to castrated master – from what we might call conservative to liberal capitalism – has left material class inequalities tragically intact. While a certain form of conservative capitalism celebrated the uncastrated master, contemporary liberal capitalism celebrates a castrated one – but both miss the point of what is needed to build an anti-capitalist social structure. True comedy does not.

At the beginning, the film shows us an uncastrated master. At a weighing scales factory, a boss locally famed for keeping his workers happy now faces a disgruntled employee protesting outside the building after his dismissal. To make the problem go away, he offers to double the worker's severance package. Back at the factory, a senior member of management is distracted and working at half-speed because his wife wants to leave him. The good boss takes the wife for coffee to convince her to stay with the husband and restore order so he can work effectively once more. Later, he makes a deal with some young thugs to keep violence in the community down. 'We know a little about balance in our business', the boss repeatedly insists, and his role is to ensure the micro society around his business maintains its equilibrium.

He does so in the role of economic and familial patriarch. With no children himself, he refers to his workers as his offspring. With senior members of staff, he insists he is a friend or a brother, rather than a boss. Flirting with a new girl taking an internship in marketing at the factory, the boss tells her that the interns are like his daughters, before starting an affair with her. Taking his manager to a strip club, he offers to pay for a lap dance to give some distraction from his divorce. While he has sex with his mistress, we see that she has a scale tattoo at the back of her neck. In this

CONCLUSION

sense he is what we might think of as a traditional conservative idea of a master – a healthy balance between virility, libido and transgression on one side of the scale and responsibility, patriarchy and economic power on the other. We might say he represents the figure of the master from a recently bygone era of capitalism, where men could be men and community structure had a degree of hierarchical security. While women and younger men might lack authority, real men enjoyed an imaginary feeling of uncastrated power.

He then becomes the castrated master. By the middle of the week, things have taken a turn. The protesting employee is getting newspaper attention in the liberal press and puts the balance of the business in jeopardy. At home his sexual affair threatens to come out and ruin the stability of family life. The mistress turns out to be a young girl he cared for as a child. An Arabic employee refuses to play ball with the boss's attempt to balance the scales. Race activism and the #MeToo movement lurk in the background of his pending demise. The times are changing, and the white, wealthy patriarchal master's function in society has changed. A pair of scales breaks.

CONCLUSION

By Friday he is totally castrated. He hides from his mistress at work and reneges on his stubbornness to offer the protesting worker whatever he wants to stop protesting, only to be rejected. His role is to be a master still, but a failed one. The mistress has better sex with the rebellious Arabic employee and publicly insults the boss, who nevertheless is now so castrated that he gives the employee sleeping with his mistress a promotion. Soon, the mistress will also manage to get into a position of power in the company by blackmailing him. Suddenly, a broken scales that stands outside the factory gates has miraculously fixed itself and balance has been restored. He becomes the embodiment of the master for a new kind of society – a society based on the decapitation of the father figure of the past in favour of upward mobility for a more diverse group of individuals. Contemporary liberal culture has taken over from traditional social and economic conservatism.

But this is not celebrated by the film, nor is it presented as a preferable situation for the community at large. The former employee decides he prefers protesting to work and commits to a life of protest and poverty for himself and his children. Protesting at night because he is so happy doing so, he is beaten up by local thugs who – back on Tuesday in traditional society – the boss had previously kept in check. The protestor tragically kills one in self-defence and the community mourns. Workers carry on with much the same inequality as before, with a powerful final scene mirroring the film's opening, as workers are forced to clap and applaud their new team of bosses, now including a young woman and an Arabic man. Class politics – and the form of the factory and its management system – remain the same, even if race and gender roles – the content of those systems – change.

On top of this, the immoral sexual transgressions that are leveraged to usher in this social revolution do not lead into a more ethical future. The capitalist boss immediately works out how to turn the new cultural situation to his advantage. To fire the manager and make way for the Arabic employee's promotion, the boss uses a #MeToo story from one of their nights in the strip club against him to blackmail him out of complaining to the union. The mistress simultaneously blackmails the boss into a job for herself, but the boss immediately turns this to his advantage by winning a long-coveted award for best boss, after

CONCLUSION

saying to a committee that he appointed her so that his company would reflect a strong female point of view. Job security is completely out of the window and the community is just as corrupt and unfulfilling – and with just as many victims – as the traditional community from the week before. Each castration cuts a master from a position of power in order to facilitate the transfer of power to another apparently uncastrated master, who steps into the phallic position – even (of course) if they might no longer be male.

The film jokes that what we need is not to castrate the wrong people and empower the right ones – the logic of contemporary capitalism and contemporary comedy – but to accept our universal castration. We could say that the film offers a mini comic history of what has happened to capitalism and its class politics in recent years. For all the positive gains made at the level of representation, the comic sadness of the film comes in that the scales of capitalism themselves remain balanced, even despite the best efforts of the culture wars. The outdated conservative model of a master might be of a virile uncastrated masculinity that secures community structure, but the liberal model of a decapitated master replaced by the younger, more diverse but just as phallic newcomer leaves nothing but raw capitalism and self-interest. The film leaves us with a sense of the need to resurrect community, structure, family and perhaps even the figure of the master, without the two inadequate versions of social life presented to us today by liberals and conservatives.

It has become a trope of liberal discourse, including among unionists and activists, to criticize the increasingly grey area between work and social life. We should be suspicious, we're told, of any member of the managerial class who appears to cultivate friendly and personal relationships, lest we become dependent on, manipulated by, or even ultimately abused, as a result of these relationships. *The Good Boss* also documents this trend. In the film, on Monday (in the era of conservative capitalism) the boss tells his employees to treat him 'not like a boss' but as a friend, brother or father but, by Thursday (in the era of contemporary liberal capitalism), he says that 'you don't get to know your employees at all'. The #MeToo narrative has fed into this movement too, pressing out the personal in favour of the professional. *The Good Boss* places this in its context of a shift in the way capitalism relates to its masters.

Both Freud and Lacan pointed out that we are all castrated – men, women, those in positions of power and those subjected to it. It is, in fact, one of the few universalizing things we might say of all subjects – no matter their race, class or gender. This universalist feature ought to be at the heart of creating any kind of political community – a community that accepts the Other in its castrated being and is able to show its own lacking subjectivity as well. It is this that would resist the capitalistic drive to turn us all into commodities who can compete with and usurp each other, and that capitalistic drive lives strongly in a contemporary culture that heralds itself as progressive and transformative, while it leaves class structures firmly in place.

Comedy – in its true form – has a neurotic *fort da* embrace/repression of castration inherent to its core. It approaches the void of existence and turns us away from it, but in doing so it points us to the universal core of a lacking and castrated subjectivity. This is why we can never be fulfilled by comedy, only shaken by it. The didactic jokes of the moment preach only to their converted

CONCLUSION

audience, confirming their inclinations and pro-
clivities, while damning those of others. Most
comedy of today operates like the characters
in de Aranoa's film, castrating one in order to
replace it with another. True comedy – like de
Aranoa's film itself, undermines this and reveals
it to be the structure of subjectivity to be and to
repress castration.

While many of today's jokes attempt to celebrate their position of the uncastrated euphorically
and with power, real comedy is marked by the
castrating detumescence of failure. In his seminar
on the logic of fantasy, Lacan describes the comic
spirit in terms of orgasm and the disillusionment
that comes with the failure of the phallic organ.

> It is insofar as it is the organ which is the seat
> of detumescence that, somewhere, the subject can
> have the illusion – a deceptive one undoubtedly,
> but even though it is deceptive it is nonetheless
> satisfying – that there is no remainder, or, at the
> very least, that there is only a perfectly vanishing
> remainder.
>
> This, in truth, might be simply of the order of the
> comic, and certainly belongs to it. (Lacan, 14, 142)

CONCLUSION

The detumescence of post-orgasm reveals the deceptive illusion of the subject's previous state of fantasy. It comically shows the subject as it is, caught up in ideology, fantasy and the pursuit of its goals but always inherently failing and confronting its universal subjective nature. One of the great jokes of all time told by Norm Macdonald mirrors the structure of orgasms:

> For the eighth year in a row Jet Blue Airlines was named the best for satisfaction. Do you know what airline was named worst for satisfaction? 9/11 Airways.

> That's a terrible name for an airline, it reminds me of that tragedy.

The first part of the joke, compact and portable in itself, builds up to its punchline and delivers what would be an affirmational joke turning on the edginess of joking about the tragedies of 9/11. At that point, it might even be considered a didactic joke insofar as joking about 9/11 represents a mockery of America and perhaps even of its foreign policy in the wake of it. Certainly, to do so is more acceptable to a contemporary

CONCLUSION

sensibility than joking about other mass murders and atrocities. The final line of the joke extends it too far and appears, as it were, after the orgasm of the joke's punchline. It states the obvious: that it would be crazy to name an airline after a terrorist aircraft attack. It is a 'vanishing remainder' – to use Lacan's terms – which leaves us in a detumescent state, calling attention to the push and pull of a joke's power. It perfectly shows the powerful ideological fantasy of a joke which can catch us in its grip and make us the subjects of ideology, but it also makes us confront this production of ideology as the deceptive illusion that it is. We are subject to the power of jokes, but the joke is always on us.

There are no good and bad jokes, because all jokes – when they are funny – contain the signal of the core of subjectivity: failure, lack, disaster and contradiction. In this sense, attempts to divide jokes into the ethical and the unethical miss the point. There are ultimately no good, ethical or universalist jokes to compare with bad, divisive or right-wing jokes, even if the examples used here have attempted to be one or other of these things. Jokes might attempt to function in one of these ways but, whatever the joke is, it is always universal, either in its contradictory status that goes against the grain of the conscious position of the joker, or in its universalist conscious approach. Only when it isn't funny can it be truly didactic, affirmative and ideological. In this sense, there is an attempt to establish a post-comedy society.

Jokes, comedy and laughter have been theorized and hypothesized endlessly by comedians, scholars, scientists and by everyone at the pub debating and engaging with friends. Since the time of Aristotle and the Greek and Roman comedies of Aristophanes and Plautus, it has been known that comedy is deeply powerful, ideological and critical to the formation and maintenance of society, even if people have always been inclined to dismiss it as unserious and apolitical.

Today, the tension around comedy is greater than ever. This is – put simply – because comedy is universalist and our society is particularist and divisive. Laughter, as we have seen, is a powerful ideological tool, which can retroactively construct, entrench and solidify identities, ideologies and truths, playing a deceptive trick that makes it appear as though we were living in a world that makes sense and has structure and order. But it also is the signal of the universal contradictory failed subjectivity from which we all originate and on top of which all ideology and fantasy is built. Our society can handle only the first of comedy's functions – its ideological force – but not its second – its universalizing instinct.

Bibliography

Baudelaire, Charles, 'On the Essence of Laughter', in *The Painter of Modern Life and Other Essays* (London: Phaidon Press, 2006), pp. 147–65.

Bakhtin, Mikhail, *Rabelais and His World*, trans. Helene Iswolsky (Bloomington: Indiana University Press, 1984).

Bakhtin, Mikhail, 'Characteristics of Genre and Plot Composition in Dostoevsky's Works' in *Fyodor Dostoevsky's Crime and Punishment*, ed. Harold Bloom (New York: Infobase, 2004), pp. 33–8.

Bown, Alfie, *In the Event of Laughter* (London: Bloomsbury, 2018).

Benjamin, Walter, *The Origin of German Tragic Drama*, trans. John Osbourne (London and New York: Verso, 2009).

BIBLIOGRAPHY

Critchley, Simon, *On Humour* (London: Routledge, 2002).

Dickens, Charles, [*GE*] *Great Expectations*, ed. Charlotte Mitchell (London: Penguin, 2003).

Dolar, Mladen, 'Strel sredi koncerta', in *Uvod v sociologijo glasbe*, ed. Theodor Adorno (Ljubljana: DZS, 1986).

Dymek, Jakub, 'Śmieszkowanie rąk nie brudzi' in *Krytika Polityczna* (30/09/2017): https://krytyka polityczna.pl/kraj/smieszkowanie-rak-nie-brudzi/

Fox, Jesse David, *Comedy Book: How Comedy Conquered Culture and the Magic That Makes It Work* (New York: Farrar, Straus and Giroux, 2023).

Freud, Sigmund, [*SE*] *The Standard Edition of the Complete Psychological Works of Sigmund Freud*, ed. and trans. James Strachey et al., 24 vols. (London: Vintage, 2001).

Frye, Northrop, *Anatomy of Criticism* (Princeton: Princeton University Press, 1957).

Goriunova, Olga, 'The Force of Digital Aesthetics: On Memes, Hacking, and Individuation', *Zeitschrift für Medienwissenschaft*, 8 (2013): 70–87.

Hall, Jonathan, *Anxious Pleasures* (London: Associated University Press, 1995).

Hegel, Georg Friedrich, *The Logic of Sense*, ed. and

trans. George di Giovanni (Cambridge: Cambridge University Press, 2010).

Kant, Immanuel, *Critique of the Power of Judgment*, trans. Paul Guyer and Eric Matthews (Cambridge: Cambridge University Press, 2000).

Kincaid, James, *Dickens and the Rhetoric of Laughter* (Oxford: Clarendon Press, 1971).

Kundera, Milan, *The Book of Laughter and Forgetting*, trans. Alan Asher (London: Faber and Faber, 1996).

Lacan, Jacques, *Seminar of Jacques Lacan 3: The Psychoses,* trans. Russell Grigg (New York: W. W. Norton, 1997).

Lacan, Jacques, *Formations of the Unconscious: Book 5: The Seminar of Jacques Lacan,* trans. Russell Grigg (London: Polity, 2017).

Lacan, Jacques, *Seminar 12: The Logic of Phantasy* (unofficial translations by Cormac Gallagher): http://www.lacaninireland.com/web/wp-content /uploads/2010/06/14-Logic-of-Phantasy-Com plete.pdf

Lefebvre, Henri, *The Critique of Everyday Life: The One-Volume Edition* (London: Verso, 2014).

Lipps, Theodor, *Komik und Humor: Eine psychologisch-asthetische* (Hamburg und Leipzig: L. Voss, 2005).

BIBLIOGRAPHY

Maleszka, Michał and Mateusz Trzeciak, 'O wartości, etykę i skuteczność', *Nowy Obywatel* (6/2/2017): http://nowyobywatel.pl/2017/02/06/o-wartosci-etyke-i-skutecznosc/

Mannoni, Octave, *Clefs pour l'Imaginaire* (Paris: Seuil, 1960).

Mauron, Charles, *Psychocritque du Genre Comique* (Paris: Libraire José Corti, 1964).

McGowan, Todd, *Only a Joke Can Save Us: A Theory of Comedy* (Evanston, IL: Northwestern University Press, 2017).

McGowan, Todd, *The Racist Fantasy* (London: Bloomsbury, 2022).

Outley, Corliss, Shamaya Bowen and Harrison Pinckney, 'Laughing While Black: Resistance, Coping and the Use of Humor as a Pandemic Pastime among Blacks', *Leisure Sciences*, 43: 1–2, 305–14. doi: 10.1080/01490400.2020.1774449 (2021).

Parker, Ian and David Pavon-Cuellar, 'Lacanian Domains of Practice and Forms of Event in Analysis', in *Lacan, Discourse, Event* (London: Routledge, 2013), pp. 338–46.

Pérez, Raúl, *The Souls of White Jokes: How Racist Humor Fuels White Supremacy* (Stanford: Stanford University Press, 2022).

BIBLIOGRAPHY

Pfaller, Robert, 'The Familiar Unknown, the Uncanny, the Comic', in *Lacan: The Silent Partners*, ed. Slavoj Žižek (London: Verso, 2005), pp. 198–296.

Rozitchner, Léon, *Freud and the Limits of Bourgeois Individualism*, trans. Bruno Bosteels (Boston: Brill, 2023).

Rzeczkowski, Grzegorz, 'Serial "Ucho prezesa": ośmiesza czy ociepla wizerunek władzy?', *Polityka* (24/09/2017): https://www.polityka.pl/tygodnik polityka/kraj/1691502,1,serial-ucho-prezesa-osmiesza-czy-ociepla-wizerunek-wladzy.read

Swales, Stephanie, *Perversion: A Lacanian Psychoanalytic Approach to the Subject* (London: Routledge, 2012).

Žižek, Slavoj, *Event: Philosophy in Transit* (London: Penguin Books, 2014).

Zupančič, Alenka, *The Odd One In* (London: MIT Press, 2008).

Zupančič, Alenka, 'Reversals of Nothing: The Case of the Sneezing Corpse', *Filozofski Vestnik*, 2 (26) (2005): 173–86.